1

The Person of Jesus

STUDIES FOR SMALL GROUPS COLLEGE
Group Study

Mark Moore
&
Jon Weece

International Standard Book Number 0-89900-847-X

TABLE
OF
CONTENTS

4

The Person of Jesus

WHO IS HE, REALLY?

We all want him as a next door neighbor—someone to care for us when we're sick and watch the house while we're away. We want him to be our confidant—one who will listen empathetically without casting aspersions on our character. We want him to be a big brother who can pull us out of a jam and give us good advice about managing life's difficulties. We want so desperately for Jesus to be all we need that we have created an imaginary friend like we did when we were children. He's somewhat of a superhero blended with Santa Claus. Or perhaps we should call this figment a drone that can be at our beck and call. But is that who he is *really*?

Can we fit him who strides the skies into our back pocket? Can we snap our fingers at the one who stills storms? Can we make demands of the Divine? Who is Jesus *really*?

Perhaps rather than creating him in our image we ought to allow him to recreate us in his. That's really what this

6 series of lessons is all about. We want to have a face-to-face encounter with a very real person rather than a mist in the mirror fogged by our own breath. If you're ready for reality rather than comfortable religious fantasy, then we welcome you to this study.

We've chosen vignettes from the gospels that open a window into the soul of the very Son of God. These incidents give us insight into who he *really* is and what he has to do with us. They take us on a pilgrimage of sorts. It begins with our presuppositions and ends with his person. Before embarking on this journey, however, you should be prepared. Normally that means packing a bunch of bags and checking off all the paraphernalia necessary when one leaves home. On this trip, however, you'll need to do just the opposite. Rather than collecting necessities, you'll need to lay them all down. To truly see Jesus requires one to strip himself of all but a pliable heart. Your aspirations and accomplishments, preconceived notions and prejudices must be abandoned. The journey takes us through several narrow passages that disallow excess baggage. In this quest for Christ we come with just ourselves. Anything more or anything less is unacceptable.

Why would one take such a trip? Oh, that's simple, really. Because in finding him we find the treasure of life which replaces the trinkets we formerly called "living." In him we find truth and healing and rest. And when we find him, we finally find our true selves.

The Person of Jesus

JESUS THE LIVING LOGOS

"The Gospel is a declaration, not a debate."
—James S. Stewart

"With the incarnation came the Man, and the addition of a new spiritual dimension to the cosmic scene. The universe provides a stage; Jesus is the play!"
—Malcolm Muggeridge

"Caesar hoped to reform men by changing institutions and laws; Christ wished to remake institutions, and lessen laws, by changing men."
—Will Durant

Text: John 1:1-18   **Memory:** John 1:12-13

All The Difference

Bill Wilson had been stabbed twice, shot at, and had a member of his team killed while working with a Sunday school ministry in a part of New York City that had been rated the "most likely place to get killed."

One Puerto Rican lady, after becoming a Christian, came to Wilson with an urgent request. She didn't speak a word of English, so she told him through an interpreter, "I want to do something for God, please."

"I don't know what you can do," Wilson answered.

"Please, let me do something," she said in Spanish.

"Okay, we'll put you on a bus. Ride a different bus every week and just love the kids."

So, every week she rode a different bus. There were fifty of them in all. She would find the worst looking kid on the bus, put him on her lap, and whisper over and over the only words she had learned in English: "I love you, and Jesus loves you."

After several months, she became attached to one little boy in particular. "I don't want to change buses anymore. I want to stay on this one bus," she said.

The boy didn't speak. He came to Sunday school every week with his sister and sat on the woman's lap, but he never made a sound. Each week she would tell him all the way to Sunday school and all the way home, "I love you and Jesus loves you."

One day, to her amazement, the little boy turned around and stammered, "I–I love you, too." Then he put his arms around her and gave her a big hug.

That was 2:30 on a Saturday afternoon. At 6:30 that night, the boy was found dead in a garbage bag under a fire escape. His mother had beaten him to death and thrown his body in the trash.

"I love you and Jesus loves you." Those were some of the last words he heard in his short life—from the lips of a Puerto Rican woman who could barely speak English.

This lesson is about another foreigner who came with the same message. Here we meet Jesus, who came to sit beside us and let us know that in a world filled with corruption and confusion, he loves us. In the midst of this mayhem he too died so that we could die knowing of his love. And that has made all the difference.

Overview of the Text

John is such a simple book. His stories are clear and his language is understandable. In fact, Greek students read John first because it is the easiest of all the New Testament books to translate. This is what you might expect from a Galilean fisherman. Yet, John's simplicity is not shallow. As this prologue demonstrates, his ideas are as deep as a thousand oceans. In these first eighteen verses, John introduces us to the Cosmic

Christ, higher than the heavens and older than the universe. This portrait of Jesus will blow your mind! It is even bigger than the vision of Christ that opens John's Revelation (1:12-18). These are *massive* ideas couched in the simplest words. Enjoy its simplicity, revel in its immensity, and just beware. This lesson really should come with a warning label: "Loitering here may cause cognitive disequilibrium."

Pondering the Person of Jesus

- Who was the first person to sit with you and share the love of Jesus?
- What comparisons could be made between Genesis 1 and John 1?
- Why does John portray Jesus as equal to God at the very beginning of the Gospel?
- What is the difference in "living" and "being alive"? What does Christ do in us or for us that makes the difference?

> **Special Note**
>
> Read through this text aloud and slowly. If a particular verse reminds you of a certain person write his or her name in the margin of your Bible. Simply show him or her this verse this week. Be prepared to report on this encounter with the group next week.

Meaning of the Text

This text is bulging with theological "stuff." It oozes ideas that beg for attention. While we can't cover all of it here, we must not miss the broad strokes of John's portrait of Jesus. *He describes him as creator God who has somehow slipped into skin.* John paints his picture with poetic language. To be specific, he uses a literary device called *chiasm*. This is where the first and the last lines match each other, the second and the next to last lines match each other, and so on. If you plot them on a piece of paper, they form a wedge-like or "greater-than" structure (" > "). It is really quite clever. This structure is important for understanding this prologue. So before moving on, take out a piece of paper and plot John's thoughts. On the left margin write out verses 1-2. Indent half an inch and write out verses 3-5, indent again and write 6-9, do it again with verses 10-11 and finally verses 12-13. Now you've come to the center of the wedge (" > "). Begin moving backward, aligning verse 14 under 10-11, verse 15 under 6-8, verses 16-17 under 3-5 and finally verse 18 under 1-2. Draw lines between specific words and phrases that are parallel.

This exercise unfolds the text before our very eyes. Each of these indentations reveals something important about Jesus. First, John says, "Jesus is God." Many Christians blithely read these words with little thought of their magnitude. John is claiming, with a straight face, that a human being has embodied *Yahweh*. That's quite an assertion coming from a Jew! But make no mistake, that is, in fact, what John is saying. Between verses 1-2 and 18 he could not have been clearer. Jesus is the "Word" (*logos*) of God. This word for "word" is rich. It didn't merely mean an oral declaration. It isn't simply a syntactical piece of a linguistic puzzle. It was a philosophical term that had woven its way through the Greek, Roman, and Jewish intellectuals. It is kind of complex but in a nutshell, *"logos" was a word from God that had somehow taken physical form in our earthly realm in order to carry out the will of God*. Whew! That's a big chunk of mental goop. Perhaps our fisherman author is not such a simpleton after all. He is articulating the incarnation in rich philosophic terms such an idea deserves. This *logos* was a will, purpose, and power of *God* embodied in the person of Jesus.

This is such a bold assertion, in fact, that John refuses to stand alone in his testimony. He elicits the support of his

The Person of Jesus

former mentor, John the Baptist (vv. 6-9,15). It is as if John the Apostle calls the Baptist to his side and says, "You tell them . . . tell them I'm speaking truth." The two venerable saints stand in unison on this critical and extraordinary declaration. Even these two, however, do not stand alone. "Doubting" Thomas cries, "My Lord and my God" (John 20:28). The Roman centurion at the cross as well as his comrade at the empty tomb called Jesus the Son of God (Mark 15:39; Matt. 27:54). The demons seconded that (Luke 4:41). Nicodemus said, "We know you have come from God" (John 3:1-2). Even Jesus said of himself, "I am the resurrection and the life" (John 11:25) and "if you have seen me you have seen the Father" (John 14:9). This is just the tip of the iceberg. The New Testament is full of claims that Jesus is God (John 1:18; 12:41; Rom. 9:5; 2 Thess. 1:12; Titus 2:13; Heb. 1:8; 2 Pet. 1:1; 1 John 5:20). While this appears to be extraordinary in the extreme, from hindsight, God did announce his coming (Isa. 9:6-7).

As if this isn't enough, John lays a second bombshell on us. Not only was Jesus *God*, he was the very one who *created* the world. (Look at vv. 3-5,16-17, the second indention in the wedge—" > "). Genesis teaches us that God created through the power of his word—he *spoke* things into existence. Theologians call this *Divine Fiat*. John declares that the *Divine Fiat* has a human face. Jesus is the very power sent forth from God to bring into existence the universe. Paul echoes this sentiment: "For by him all things were created: things in heaven and on earth, visible and invisible, whether thrones or powers or rulers or authorities; all things were created by him and for him" (Col. 1:16). Here's where it gets interesting. The Genesis creation account describes God as creator of life and light. That's exactly what Jesus brings (v. 4)! However, the new creation of John 1 is quite different from the original creation of Genesis. This life and light are not physical but spir-

Jesus the Living Logos

12 itual. When verse four says that Jesus brings life, the Greek word is *zoe*. John could have used the word *bios*, indicating biological life. Or he could have used *psuche*, indicating the presence of a living *soul*. Both of these were part of the original creation. The new creation gives us life at a much deeper level. This *zoe* kind of life is what John describes as "eternal life" throughout his book. What's the difference? You can tell if a person has *bios* by listening for a heartbeat. You can tell if she has *psuche* by looking in her eyes. But *zoe* comes from the lips—it is heard in laughter and song. It is life that wells up from the deepest part of us and explodes onto the earthly plane. It is our passion and purpose, our vision and dance. *Bios* and *psuche* merely support life, *zoe* is the reason for living.

How does Jesus recreate us with this depth of life? Look again at your chiasm chart. What is parallel to this new creation of verses 3-5? Verses 16-17 describe how *zoe* comes. It is through grace. In other words, the law of God was retired by the sacrifice of Christ (Col. 2:13-14). The phrase "one blessing after another" could be translated "one blessing in place of another." In fact, that makes more sense in light of verse 17. The blessing of Moses was the law. It opened up a relationship with God for an entire nation. In Christ, however, the law has been replaced with grace, which opens up a better relationship with God for the entire world.

This leads us to the third and final bombshell of John's prologue. This cosmic creator somehow had compassion on this minute particle called earth. He loved his rebellious creation, his fallen trophy. In a mystery we shall never understand, our omnipotent God squeezed himself into the smallest fragment of skin (vv. 10,14). Now comes the tragedy: We didn't recognize him. "He was in the world, and though the world was made through him, the world did not recognize him. He came to that which was his own, but his own did not receive him"

The Person of Jesus

(vv. 10-11). The scandal of this insurrection is more revolting **13**
than any treacherous act in human history.

So what will come of all this? If you have been tracing
our pilgrimage across the chiasm, you see that we have come
to the point of the " > ." The way this literary device works is
that the point is *the point*. This single sentence (vv. 12-13) will
answer this crucial question: What will result from the incarnation? One might expect God to come and wreak havoc on
a rebellious humanity. After all, all kinds of religious stories
from Greek mythology to the Babylonian epics describe the
gods decimating mortal ingrates.

In a surprise twist, however, when Yahweh comes for a
visit, we are granted the legal authority to become children of
God. We can actually be adopted into the Divine family with
all its rights and privileges. And he did more than sit down
next to us on the bus. He became like us and spoke in a language we can all understand; it's the language of love. Surely
this is the most extraordinary revelation of this entire text,
greater even than the incarnation. It is shocking enough that
God came to us. It is overwhelming that we could be with him.

Imitating the Person of Jesus

1. Call a friend who has adopted a child.
   1) Make two lists from your conversation:
      a) The necessary steps in the adoption process
      b) Joys and difficulties in bringing an outsider into your family
   2) Now write down your own observations of how these are similar
      to what God has done for you.
2. Use this previous exercise as a foundation for an extended time of
   prayer with God (30-60 minutes) in which you talk to God about your
   relationship.

2 GREAT 2 COSMIC POWERS IN AN ITTY-BITTY LIVING 2 SPACE 2

> "He became what we are that He might make us what He is."
> —Athanasius

> "Alexander, Caesar, Charlemagne, and I myself have founded great empires . . .
> But Jesus alone founded His empire upon love, and to this very day, millions would die for Him. Jesus Christ was more than a man."
> —Napoleon

Text: Luke 1:26-56   **Memory:** Luke 1:30-33

Blind to the Good News A bishop from the East Coast paid a visit many years ago to a small, midwestern religious college. He stayed at the home of the college president, who also served as professor of physics and chemistry. After dinner, the bishop declared that the millennium couldn't be far off, because just about everything about nature had been discovered and all inventions conceived. The young college president politely disagreed and said he felt there would be many more discoveries. When the angered bishop challenged the president to name just one such invention, the president replied he was certain that within fifty years men would be able to fly.

"Nonsense!" Sputtered the outraged bishop. "Only angels are intended to fly."

The bishop's name was Wright, and he had two boys at

home who would prove to have greater vision than their father. Their names: Orville and Wilbur.

When these two boys made their historic flight at Kitty Hawk, they sent a short telegram home to their sister that read: "First sustained flight. 59 seconds. Be home for Christmas." Their sister was so thrilled by the news, that she took the telegram to the local newspaper editor. He read it with interest and the next day printed this headline: Famous Bicycle Manufacturers Will Be Home for Christmas.

Not only is a lack of vision dangerous, so is the denial of the good news a messenger brings to your attention. Mary is not such a person. She accepts the news brought by the angelic messenger thereby allowing us to see a heart with a passion for God's plan.

Overview of the Text

Mary has been hailed as the mother of God by millions. Rosary beads rattle her name; icons perpetuate her image. In reaction to inappropriate adoration, Protestants have often imprudently ignored her contribution. In this lesson we want to listen carefully to this teen queen. Through her eyes, we can see Jesus with unparalleled clarity.

Pondering the Person of Jesus

✵ What do you think were some of the very real consequences Mary had to deal with due to this miraculous conception?

✵ Men, what would be your response if your fiancee was chosen by God to bear the Christ?

✵ Why do you think it was important that God met humanity in a bodily form?

✵ What indications are there that Jesus was fully human?

Meaning of the Text

Luke writes his birth narrative like a soap opera that flips back and forth

Cosmic Powers in an Itty-bitty Space

between scenes. In the opening scene this great angel of Daniel 9 appears in the Holy Place to the old man Zechariah. He reveals the coming miraculous birth of John. This second scene (Luke 1:26) opens six months later. Gabriel shows up in a humble village in Galilee with a similar revelation to a teenage girl. She too would have a son; he too would be God's man and be named by the angel. Only now the stakes are higher. It is one thing for an elderly couple to conceive after menopause. All the neighbors clap their hands and squeal in delight. It is quite another thing for a young woman in the middle of her engagement to wind up pregnant, claiming she's still a virgin. All the neighbors shake their fingers and speak in whispered tones.

The stakes are higher in another way too. John was to be a prophetic figure crying in the wilderness. Jesus was to be a king leading his people to liberation. He will reinstall David's kingdom and usher Yahweh back into Jerusalem. Those are large sandals to fill. Mary is young, but she is not naive. She understands both the glory and the cost of Gabriel's announcement. As her poem will demonstrate, she knows a good bit about the Old Testament. Thus Gabriel's words cause a cascade of thoughts. Passage after passage ricocheted through her synapses, exploding into this question: "How can this be since I am a virgin?" Gabriel gives her an answer "The Holy Spirit." He also gives her some supporting evidence in her elder relative Elizabeth. Mary accepts the revelation as well as its risks and responsibilities. In fact, when she says, "May it be to me . . ." (v. 38), the words imply a wish or a desire. It is kind of like when we say, "May God bless you." In other words, Mary willingly submitted to God's dangerous plan for her life. At the very real risk of divorce, social ostracism, and even potential execution, Mary receives in her body the plan and power of God.

With her head still spinning, she packs her bags and is on her way. We don't know if her parents went with her on the seventy-mile trek to Judea. But off she goes to witness the evidence offered by the angel. Within a week she is on her kinswoman's doorstep. Without e-mail or telegrams it is unlikely Elizabeth knew she was coming or why. Yet John, still three months premature, started skipping in the womb when they met. This was John's cue to his mother that something special was happening. The Holy Spirit fleshed out the revelation John's little ditty introduced. Consequently, Elizabeth shouts out the earliest declaration of the deity of Jesus while he was yet a blastula.

This is all quite splendid but we're not done yet. Elizabeth is not the only one with a pious confession. Mary has composed an entire poem. That is impressive since she was likely illiterate and more impressive given the fact that this poem has over a dozen phrases that point to Old Testament texts. In other words, this pious, poor peasant has listened carefully from the fringes of the synagogue. Her ears and heart absorbed the Torah she never laid eyes on. Likely it was during her three- to four-day journey to Judea that she mulled over Gabriel's announcement and laced it together with OT allusions. This poem is as pregnant with Scripture as Mary is with the Holy Spirit.

There is something else interesting about this passage. It is feminine poetry. That places it in a small but significant category of biblical literature. We have Miriam's song of celebration as the Israelites cross the Red Sea and witness their enemies' demise (Exod. 15). Then there is Deborah's song of celebration after the defeat of the Midianites (Judg. 5). Finally, Hannah chimes in when her barrenness is reversed (1 Sam. 2).

It is odd that these words come from Mary's lips at all. For example, this poem echoes Hannah's, yet Hannah's condition is really closer to Elizabeth's than to Mary's. Moreover, both Miriam and Deborah sing of war not birth. In addition,

Cosmic Powers in an Itty-bitty Space

18 as we read Mary's song, we soon realize that it too has little to do with cradles and swaddling clothes. It has a lot to do with the defeat of God's enemies as he liberates the poor. Mary has a better handle on what's going on than most of us at Christmastime. This is not a quaint little Christmas carol. It is a military march to be accompanied by bass drums and cymbals.

One last note before we look at the actual text. Mary's poem is excellent Hebrew poetry. It has the classic parallelism and is teeming with scriptural allusions. However, we don't have a copy of it in Hebrew (or Aramaic). It comes to us in Greek and fine Greek at that. Apparently Luke took Mary's poem and translated it in his own language with excellence that matched the original. It really is quite a piece of literature and the only feminine touch in the whole New Testament. For that it should be cherished.

Mary's song has three stanzas. The first speaks of how God has been gracious to her (vv. 46-49). The second tells of God's graciousness to all the humble (i.e., the poor and disenfranchised) (vv. 50-53). Finally, it encompasses all of Israel (vv. 54-55). In other words, the poem begins with Mary and branches out to the entire nation. Mary is thus a representative of the poor who turn out to be the true citizens of God's kingdom. This seems exceedingly strange in light of their predicament. They are not living as royalty but paupers. Thus the theme of the song, which spreads like a banner across the whole, is "reversal." Things are not as they should be. But very soon Yahweh will intervene. When he installs his soon-coming kingdom, things will be turned upside down so they can once again be right-side up. Had this piece been published in a tabloid in Jerusalem, you can be sure that the powers that be would have raised an eyebrow if not a sword. This is subversive talk with very real implications to the social order of the day. Mary is not simply a sweet little girl that qui-

The Person of Jesus

etly submitted to God's will. Her song shouts. It throws down
a gauntlet and establishes a pattern that her son will carry to
completion.

Imitating the Person of Jesus

1. Fill in the following chart, "What Mary Knew about Baby Jesus":

Informant	Text	Information
	Luke 1:31-35	1. 2. 3. 4. 5. 6. 7.
	Luke 1:43	8.
	Luke 1:48-55	9. 10.
	Matt 1:20-23	11. 12. 13.
	Luke 2:11	14.
	Luke 2:26-35	15. 16. 17. 18. 19.
	Luke 2:38	20.
	Isaiah 9:6-9	21. 22. 23. 24.

2. After doing the first exercise as a group, take some time to write a one-page declaration of who you believe Jesus is and what you believe he will do. If you dare, make it poetic as Mary's was. Take about 10 minutes for this exercise and share your results with the group.

Cosmic Powers in an Itty-bitty Space

3

THE BAPTISM OF JESUS

3   **3**

3   **3**

> "In baptism, the direction
> is indicated rather
> than the arrival."
> —Friedrich Rest

Text: Matthew 3:13-17 & Mark 1:9-13   **Memory:** Mark 1:9-11

Delayed Freedom   Toward the end of World War II, two pilots—a Scottish chaplain and a professor from Glasgow—were shot down behind enemy lines. German soldiers quickly captured them and led them to a nearby prison camp. The camp was separated into two sections. One barracks housed American soldiers and the other housed British soldiers. For some reason the two British pilots were separated and one was placed among the American soldiers.

Every day the two men would meet at a wire fence that separated the allied troops and exchange greetings. Unknown to the guards, the Americans had a small homemade radio and they were able to get news from the outside, something more precious than food in a prison camp. The professor would share a headline or two with his friend who in turn would share it with their fellow British soldiers. They knew the allied forces were advancing, getting closer and closer to victory.

One day news came over the radio, announcing that the German high command had surrendered and the war was over. The professor took the news to the fence, then stood and watched as his friend disappeared into the British barracks. Moments later, a roar of celebration came from within the British housing unit. When the German guards finally heard the news, three nights later, they fled in the dark, leaving the gates unlocked. The next morning, the British and American troops walked out as free men, although they had truly been set free three days earlier by the news that the war was over.

In the story of Jesus' baptism, we glimpse a battle of the war Jesus waged against sin. The ground he claimed that day was not in the physical realm, rather he determined the course of his life and the future of

Overview of the Text   our souls.

There he stands in the middle of the Jordan with a drenched camel hair coat, dunking the masses. People come from the four corners of the country to listen to this wild-eyed prophet screaming something about an incoming kingdom. They respond with repentance in a burial rite of sorts. This motley crew includes the poor with hopes for a brighter future and the religious leaders with questions about John's intentions and identity. There are even Roman peacekeeping forces, hated for their extortion and brutality. They too ask to join. From the midst of the crowd steps Jesus, John's relative and six months his younger. He also asks to submit to John's baptism. Now that puts John in an awkward position. Jesus is clearly his superior. Yet he asks for John's ritual washing. Truly this was a curious encounter.

The Baptism of Jesus

- Read Romans 6:3-6. Explain how immersion pictures and preaches the gospel in a nutshell. Is it possible that Jesus' baptism is an enacted prophecy? In other words, do you think that it might look forward to the cross as our own baptism looks back to the cross?
- Read through the parallel accounts of Jesus' baptism and make a list of all the indications that this was a *huge* event for Jesus. What do you think it meant to Jesus? How is this an appropriate inauguration into his Messianic ministry?
- What do you think John the Baptist would have known about Jesus and expected from him? Remember, they did not live in the same town and John's parents were very old when he was born.

Meaning of the Text

Jesus came to John to receive his baptism. What are we to make of this? After all John was baptizing people as an initiation into the nascent kingdom of God. Furthermore, this immersion was for the forgiveness of their sins (Mark 1:4). (That happens to be the very same phrase used in Acts 2:38!) Jesus didn't need to do that . . . at least that's what John thought. Jesus, for his part, said that he did need to be baptized in order to fulfill all righteousness. But how does Jesus' baptism do that?

Some have suggested Jesus' baptism was merely an example for us to follow, not for forgiveness of sins. In other words, Jesus is submitting to God's plan through John the Baptist. As such, it is a great example for us to follow. If Jesus, who didn't need baptism, carried through with it, how much more should we, who so desperately need cleansing, submit to immersion?

Well, that is one way of looking at this event. Yet there seems to be something deeper here than a stellar example to follow. After all, the event will be marked by the tearing open of the heavens, the physical descent of the Holy Spirit, and the very voice of God, "This is my beloved Son . . ." This is not merely an example for future generations, this is Jesus' own inauguration. It looks for all the world like Jesus is beginning his ministry here. All four Gospel writers refer to this event (which is quite rare). This *must* be more than a mere example. Besides, if Jesus was baptized when he didn't really need to be, it makes it somewhat of a farce, kind of like parents pretending to be asleep to get their toddler to settle down.

What if this really does have something to do with the inauguration of the kingdom? What if Jesus was baptized, like everyone else, for the forgiveness of sins? "NO WAY!" You say. "Jesus had no sins to repent from!" True, but in the Jewish world, leaders *did* repent for the sins of their people—sins that they themselves did not commit. Daniel repented for the sins of his people (Dan. 9:4-18). Likewise, Nehemiah fasted for the sins of Jerusalem. Jeremiah, Ezra, and Ezekiel all took personal responsibility for the sins of their countrymen. Such is the role of prophets, priests, and kings.

If Jesus is doing that here, then several things come into focus. First, his baptism is what it looks like—repentance in preparation for the incoming kingdom. This would also make sense in the grand scheme of Jesus' ministry. After all, he also ended his ministry by taking on the sins of his people. This would make his baptism and crucifixion substitutionary book ends to his ministry. Mark seems to hint at this with his interesting word "torn open" (*schizo*) in verse 10. He only uses that word one other time in his Gospel. It is when he describes the temple curtain being torn from top to bottom. If this is deliberate, then Mark wants you to connect these two events. Christian baptism is all about the *cross* of Christ, why not also Jesus' own *immersion*?

A second thing that comes into focus is the inaugural

The Baptism of Jesus

nature of Jesus' baptism. Think about it. Jesus is not merely setting a fine example for future generations. He is making a bold declaration to the people then present at the Jordan River. He is claiming to be the leader of his people, the next great prophet and king. He is asserting his authority in no uncertain terms. Such a bold declaration needs suitable support. Jesus gets it from none other than God. The Holy Spirit makes an appearance that looked something like a dove flitting down from the sky (v. 10). Was this something that others could see? Yes, of course! John, in fact, points to this as the deciding factor of his Messianic appointment (John 1:32-34). As if that weren't enough, Yahweh speaks from heaven, "You are my Son, whom I love; with you I am well pleased." This only happened three times in Jesus' ministry and only at critical points. So the Trinity converges at the river to announce the new age dawning, not merely to applaud a noble act of obedience. Furthermore, with these words Yahweh quotes himself from Psalm 2, which is another bold announcement of the Messianic king.

This is important for the Christian to understand. We have often missed the red carpet of Jesus' baptism. We need to grasp who Jesus is through this event. Moreover, we have also missed the meaning of baptism for Christians. Obviously, the meaning of Jesus' baptism is different than ours in that we repent for our own sins. Yet our submission to immersion is like his in at least two significant ways. First, it is an inaugural event. It is not merely a noble act of obedience; it has to do with forgiveness of sins (Acts 2:38; 1 Pet. 3:21) and entering into a covenant relationship with God (Col. 2:11-12). Second, like Jesus' baptism, the Trinity converges in our own baptism (Matt. 28:19). The perfect living in the imperfect! All of us, who have been confined to the prison camp of sin, can be free. No longer do we have to stand with the fences of anger, adultery, and abuse between God and us. The prison

The Person of Jesus

doors have been opened for the single mom, the recovering alcoholic, the divorcee, the rebellious youth, and the worry-ridden senior adult. All can now exit the prison free and victorious. The war within can end! This is a powerful gift God has lavished on us.

Imitating the Person of Jesus

Share with the group what your own baptism has meant to you.

If you have not been immersed into Christ are there questions about it you would like to ask? Is there something keeping you from imitating Jesus in this way? Would you like to be immersed now? . . . I mean now!

The Baptism of Jesus

4   4

THE
TEMPTATION
OF
JESUS

4   4

Text: Matthew 4:1-11   Memory: Matthew 4:4

Perspective   In December 1914, a great sweeping fire
destroyed Thomas Edison's laboratories in
West Orange, New Jersey, wiping out two million dollars'
worth of equipment and the record of much of his life's work.
Edison's son Charles ran about frantically trying to find his
father. Finally he came upon him, standing near the fire, his
face shown in the glow of the fire, white hair blown by the
winter winds. Charles said when he saw his dad his heart
ached for him. He was no longer young and everything he
had dreamed of and worked for in life was being destroyed.

But Thomas Edison had different thoughts going
through his mind. He told his son to find his mom and bring
her to the fire's edge. "She will never see anything like this
again," Edison smiled and said.

The next morning, walking about the charred embers of

so many of his hopes and dreams, the sixty-seven-year-old Edison said, "There is great value in disaster. All of our mistakes are burned up. Thank God we can start anew!"

Overview of the Text

This is a killer fight. In one corner is the Devil, Satan, Ye Olde Tempter (all three of these titles are actually used in this text, although I added the "Ye Olde" part). In the other corner we have Jesus, the Messiah, the newly inaugurated King of Yahweh. They go head to head. Jesus is at a severe disadvantage having fasted for the last forty days. These temptations are not your ordinary, run-of-the-mill enticements. We're not talking about a little white lie or slapping your younger sister when Mom's not looking. This is all-out war. Satan is attacking Jesus at the point of contact. He is offering him a crown without a cross, a kingdom without human suffering. It is not that Satan is seducing Jesus away from his global quest of humanity. He is merely offering him a shortcut—an easier path to success. Satan is suggesting that Jesus can do it his way, which is adverse to God's. The stakes are colossal . . . even galactic.

Pondering the Person of Jesus

- How vulnerable was Jesus to Satan's attacks? Was it hard for him to resist?
- What temptation has God recently helped you overcome?
- What spiritual battles are being waged within you that need to be addressed and fought?
- Is Scripture memorization a discipline you have developed in your battle plan against the Devil?

Meaning of the Text

The scene takes place in a desert, that barren wasteland of Judea. Jesus, still dripping from baptism, is thrust into the wilderness by the Holy Spirit (cf. Mark 1:12). That gentle dove on his shoulder soon became a heavy hand in the small of his back. There he sat for forty days with nothing to chew on but his own thoughts. The Devil waited and watched. Jesus was all alone except for the wild animals that brave the harsh environs of the desert (Mark 1:13). It is a hostile environment that's about to heat up considerably.

Three times Jesus is accosted by the devil. It is interesting that these three temptations can be laid next to Eve's in Eden as well as John's assessment of the temptations of the world (1 John 2:15-17). There the elder Apostle says, "Do not love the world or anything in the world. If anyone loves the world, the love of the Father is not in him. For everything in the world—the cravings of sinful man, the lust of his eyes and the boasting of what he has and does—comes not from the Father but from the world." In short, John summarizes human temptations under three banners: Lust of the flesh, lust of the eyes, and the boastful pride of life. Let's place Jesus and Eve next to these:

1 John 2:15-17	Lust of the Flesh	Lust of the Eyes	Boastful Pride of Life
Eve	Good for Food	Delight to the eyes	Desirable to make one wise
Jesus	Stone to Bread	Kingdoms of the World	Throw yourself from the Temple

Obviously these categories are not exact. Nonetheless they are close enough to come to this conclusion: Just as Eve (and thus Adam) is a model of moral failure, Jesus is a model of spiritual resistance. There is an "undoing," in this text, of the fall. It is the same song, with a very different second verse. Jesus is not merely reenacting Adam and Eve's demise. He stands for all of us. We too find ourselves with the Serpent in the wilderness, chasing after a higher position with a better view that will put more bread in the bank.

The Person of Jesus

Now, Jesus can't claim to experience exactly what each of us has had to endure. His parents were not divorced, he was not sexually abused, he never filed for bankruptcy, he did not see his house or life's work go up in smoke, or any other number of catastrophic life experiences. In that sense, no one else can claim to understand your personal pain. Nevertheless, it would be outrageously egotistical to say you are the only one who has ever felt abandoned, lonely, sad, or overwhelmed. In fact, in every major category of sin, Jesus experienced the very same thing you have. The writer of Hebrews puts it this way: "For we do not have a high priest who is unable to sympathize with our weaknesses, but we have one who has been tempted in every way, just as we are—yet was without sin" (Heb. 4:15).

Not only do these temptations demonstrate that Jesus walked where we walk, but they show us the way through. Each time Satan tempted him, Jesus resisted by quoting Scripture. This is instructive for those of us who struggle to best the Devil. As Paul says in Ephesians 6, the Bible is our sword in spiritual battle. In fact, it is the only offensive weapon Paul lists. Now it is a wonderful thing to wear the helmet of salvation. It is a great comfort to lift high the shield of faith. But all these can do is ward off the flaming arrows of the evil one. They do not put him to flight. In other words, if you are biblically illiterate you have only defensive weapons against the Devil. Oh sure, your salvation is still secure in your armament. Yet you will be reduced to standing your ground and letting Satan beat the bejeebers out of you. If you want to ward off his attack, you'll need to wield a sword, *the* Sword.

Having said that, we must clarify something here. On the one hand, this text *is* a good model for how to overcome temptations. Indeed, Jesus has been tempted in all ways as we have. On the other hand, his temptations are qualitatively different from ours. Satan is not seducing him to some per-

The Temptation of Jesus

sonal peccadillo. He is tempting him to an alternate path. "There is an easier way," Satan says. "You don't have to submit to Yahweh's grueling incarnation."

Let's consider for example the temptation to turn a stone into bread. If I were to do that in the desert, it would be marveled as a miracle. So why is it suddenly a sin if Jesus does it? If I were to fly from the pinnacle of the temple, the video would be worth millions on CNN. So why is it so evil for Jesus? The answer is simple. All three of these temptations (bread, temple, and kingdoms) would result in Jesus' instant recognition as Messiah, yet one of the wrong sort. Remember how the crowds wanted to make Jesus king after he multiplied the loaves at the feeding of the 5,000 (John 6:15)? That was because one of the common expectations of the Messiah was his institution of a social welfare program. He would revitalize the prosperity of the nation. In short, people would be well fed. Boy oh boy, if you could turn every rock in Palestine into a loaf it would be a boon for sure!

Likewise, people expected the Messiah to appear with a sudden miraculous sign from the sky. A divine bungee jump in the Portico of Solomon would certainly fit the bill. Moreover, if Satan just handed over the kingdoms without a further fight, how much easier this incarnation stuff would be for Jesus. The issue was not a personal sin but a divine destiny. Would Jesus carry out his Messianic ministry God's way or Satan's? Would difficult obedience or seductive shortcuts characterize his life? The answer is blatantly obvious (though no less difficult). Jesus must win this battle. If he doesn't, then the cross is defunct.

When the dust settled, angels came and ministered to Jesus. This is reminiscent of another wildernessque brawl yet to come. That one would take place in a garden. There the angels return one last time to succor the Savior (Luke 2:43).

The Person of Jesus

That battle will be even fiercer than this one and the stakes will be higher. In fact, somebody's gonna bleed. How terrible it is . . . how wonderful indeed! Through Jesus' loss we're offered a fresh start.

Imitating the Person of Jesus

1. Develop an accountability system with a close friend.

    1) On a notecard, list expectations you want met from this relationship.

    2) List questions you want your accountability partner to ask you when you get together and create a confidentiality contract so that what is said between you stays between you.

    3) Set up a regular time to meet. Be honest with one another! This partnership will help you weather many storms in life!

2. In light of Jesus' temptation, plan for a 40-hour fast. During this time, lay your temptations before him and search the Scriptures to find passages that will arm you in this battle against the Devil. If you've never fasted before, consult your minister for some practical helps. This is a marvelous spiritual discipline that will infuse your faith with new avenues of worship.

5   5

THE PARTY BEGINS

5   5

Text: John 2:1-11   Memory: John 2:11

The Ultimate Party

Former President Teddy Roosevelt was known for his safari treks into the wilderness of Africa. After killing more game than his hunting party could possibly carry home, Roosevelt and his entourage decided the time had come to call it a trip and head home. They boarded a large sea vessel headed to New York. Little did he know, or anyone else on the ship for that matter, that an elderly man who had given thirty years of his life as a missionary in Africa was a passenger as well.

It was a lengthy voyage and the crew of the ship threw one party after another to honor the President. The missionary watched and listened as people ranted and raved about this special passenger. When the ship finally docked in the harbor of New York City, a crowd of thousands had gathered to welcome Roosevelt home. Bands played, people cheered,

and ticker tape was tossed. The missionary stepped off the
ship, stood nearby with his only earthly possession, a single
suitcase, and began to feel sorry for himself. He thought,
"Thirty years I have labored for the kingdom. I've battled
sickness and loneliness, and I've watched countless people
surrender to the Lordship of Jesus Christ, and not one person
is here to welcome me home." It was at that moment that he
sensed a reassuring peace unlike any he had ever known.
And he said it was as if he could hear God whispering, "But
you're not home yet. You're not home yet."

Norman Cousins once wrote, "The tragedy of life is not
in the fact of death but in what dies inside us while we live."
Hope, true hope, can seem distant and unattainable in a
world filled with empty celebrations. But Jesus has shown us,
even in the little details, that he is in control of the party and
the ending is something worth living for. Don't let that hope
die inside of you while you live!

Overview of the Text

Unlike the Synoptics, John doesn't
overwhelm his readers with a
plethora of miracles. In fact, he records only seven. This should
raise the brow of the attentive reader. You see, seven is symbol-
ic for John. In Revelation, it pops up all over the place. It has
something to do with fullness, particularly in reference to super-
natural interaction in the human realm. Thus, John's seven miracles are more than historical recollections. They are carefully
chosen vignettes that preach about the kingdom of God. More
specifically, they lead us step by step into discipleship. It begins
here with the initial invitation. We have a wedding and a barrel
of wine. These foreshadow the destiny of the believer.

Pondering the Person of Jesus

✳ In what ways do you find celebration in Christianity?
In other words, what makes you truly joyful about
being in Christ?

The Party Begins

✳ Conversely, in what ways do you find that Christians often rob joy from others rather than offer it? How is the church a "kill-joy"?

✳ With your own words and imagination, describe what you think the wedding feast will be like when Jesus returns.

✳ How does a Christian view of God differ from a Buddhist? Muslim? New Ager?

Meaning of the Text   Our story opens with this notice: "On the third day." The third day after what? Well, it was apparently the third day after they left Judea to go up north (1:43). That's where Cana was. On the one hand, the third day means practically nothing. On the other hand, it means almost everything. Put these three days in your pocket and save them for later.

Jesus & Co. arrive in this small village nestled in the hills of Galilee. Mary is there as well. In fact, she is helping the family with preparations. We don't really know what her relationship to the family was, but we do know something of the dynamics of that relationship. We need to travel back in time to see it clearly. In those days weddings were more than a storybook ceremony topped with mints and nuts. They lasted for days and were filled with feasts. The reason weddings were so significant is because they were functionally alliances between two families, not merely "twitterpation" between two lovers. So the families had to come together to show their loyalty to each other. A number of things happened in the process. For instance, the woman brought into the marriage a dowry that would show fidelity to her husband. Likewise, the husband proved his financial stability by throwing a banquet for the clan. In other words, he was proving, through the feast, that he had the wherewithal to take care of his wife and the many children they hoped to have. Now, if either side failed, that was not merely a social *faux* the plot thickens.

The wedding party has just opened their last jug of *Mogen David.* The servant girls were responsible for serving such refreshments. When they notice they are out, they realize their master is in trouble. Undoubtedly one of them goes to Mary and asks for help. First, Mary is in a position to help. Although she is likely a widow by now, her son is a rising rabbi with a significant entourage. Surely they have enough petty cash in the apostolic purse to purchase a case of cheap wine. Second, Mary is not only in a position to help but to raise her family's status. In those days, social interactions were based upon patron/client relationships. If Mary provides for this family, she would become their patron and they would be socially indebted to her family. Widows rarely had such a valuable opportunity. Third, Mary would feel comfortable making this request. Hebrew boys were supposed to be beholden to their mommas. Besides, Jesus has been gallivanting around Judea for the last nine months. This left his half-brothers to run the carpentry shop. It is about time he returned to his nuclear family and did them a favor.

This presents Jesus with a problem. Does he follow the Torah and honor his earthly mother? Or should he be led by the Spirit and honor his Heavenly Father? If he listens to Mary, he retreats back into his family; if he follows his call, he presses onward unto the kingdom. In one dramatic turn he will do both. These six stone jars hold upwards of 180 gallons of water used for ceremonial washing. After filling them to the brim with water, the servants take a sample of the contents to the master of ceremonies. He is taken by the quality of the wine, especially this late in the game.

John concludes the story by noting that this was Jesus' first miracle. It caused his disciples to put their faith in him. If we are correct that these seven signs are pictures of life in

The Party Begins

the kingdom, then what are we to see in this story? The obvious metaphors are water, wine, and weddings. In John, water is a libation of *cleansing*. Wine is a symbol of *celebration*. And the wedding is the disciple's *destiny*. In other words, when we first meet Jesus, we are invited to a wedding filled with celebration. We're not talking about a few party poppers and a kazoo. We're talking about 180 gallons of wine! That's enough blessing to bathe in! Listen friend, our invitation is to unmitigated joy and rampant rejoicing. Oh, the kingdom involves much more than this. Nonetheless, the first portrait of life in the kingdom is drawn with the colors of a party.

What if your Christian life is marked with shades of gray rather than joy? Does this mean you're a bad Christian? Well, honestly, that's a possibility. Sometimes our own stubbornness, weakness, or rebellion mitigates God's blessing. But sometimes the world just stinks. Bad stuff happens even to the innocent. Saints too have scars. So what does this text say then? There is one more metaphor that speaks to us. Pull it out of your pocket. It comes from verse one. There is a third day. That's the day when Jesus rose, the day death died. That's the day of lilies and empty tombs. It's a day of wonder and resurrection. It's a day of hope and homecomings. And the third day . . . well that's the day of weddings (Rev. 19:7). Prepare your white dress; your wedding day is coming quickly. The wine is about to flow in excess.

Imitating the Person of Jesus

1. Find a set of wedding vows. Read them aloud and think about each promise being made between the two individuals.
2. Now apply them to your relationship with God. Create a new set of vows based on the promises he has declared in your presence and the promises you have declared in his. Renew those vows in prayer.

OLD MEN AND NEW BIRTHS

> "He may try to be a secret disciple; but it has been well said that to be a secret disciple is impossible because either 'the discipleship kills the secrecy, or the secrecy kills the discipleship.'"
> —William Barclay

Text: John 3:1-21   **Memory:** John 3:19-21

Leaving Our Shells

From time to time, lobsters have to leave their shells in order to grow. They need the shell to protect them from being torn apart, yet when they grow, the old shell must be abandoned. If they do not abandon it, the old shell will soon become their prison—and eventually their casket.

The tricky part for the lobster is the brief period of time between when the old shell is discarded and the new one is formed. During that terribly vulnerable period, the transition is scary to the lobster. Currents cartwheel them from coral to kelp. Hungry schools of fish are ready to make them a part of their food chain. For a while at least, that old shell, that source of security, looks pretty good.

We are not so different from lobsters. To change and grow, we must sometimes shed our old shells—a structure, a framework, a way of life—we've depended on. Discipleship means being so committed to Christ that when he bids us to follow, we will change, risk, grow, and leave our old "shells" behind.

Overview of the Text

For all our talk about grace, we still feel that certain people have a leg up into heaven. We act as if some folks just have the right stuff—a pedigree, an education, and certain notches on their spiritual belt. In short, they are more important to God because they are more recognized by men. This text wipes away such a myth. Nicodemus, on the fast track of Sanhedrin fame, finds he too must be born again to enter the kingdom. He expects Jesus to hail him as an insider, only to be rebuffed as ignorant. This story is shocking, even offensive, for those of us who were weaned on a pew.

Pondering the Person of Jesus

- Read carefully through the text, making two lists. In the first, enumerate all the clues that Nicodemus is a good guy. In the second, collect all the indications that he is a poor disciple of Jesus.
- List your own "pedigree as a Christian." What are you doing that would make you look like a good Christian in the eyes of others? What do you think Jesus would have to say about all that (both good and bad)?
- What aspect of discipleship do you find most difficult?
- Jesus jumps on Nicodemus for not understanding spiritual rebirth. What should he have known?

Meaning of the Text

What do you do with a guy like Nicodemus? On the one hand you really want to like him. After all, he is the only Sanhedrin member who ever came to Jesus to talk about joining the ranks of the disciples. Furthermore, he gets better the deeper into the book we go. In John 7:50-51 he defends Jesus' right to a fair trial knowing he'll take a beating for it. Then in 19:39 he actually helps Joseph of Arimathea bury the crucified remains of our Lord. He looks like a good guy, but never fully follows Jesus. What do you do with a guy like that? Let's tinker with this text a bit and see if we can't draw a conclusion to that question. Pull out the lists you produced a few minutes ago and compare it to these:

Positive Attributes of Nicodemus

✝ He is a member of the Sanhedrin. That means he is an elder statesman probably over 65 years old. He drips with clout and oozes heritage. "Revered" is not too strong a word to describe his social standing in Israel.

✝ He is a Pharisee. As such he was a staunch defender of conservative Judaism and a teacher of the Bible (OT). He knew, followed, and enforced the laws of Moses.

✝ He comes to Jesus recognizing who he is. He declared, "Rabbi, we know you are a teacher who has come from God. For no one could perform the miraculous signs you are doing if God were not with him." Not bad. He had not only looked for the coming Messiah but is now honestly investigating Jesus to see if he could be the one.

✝ As mentioned earlier, he continued to stand up for Jesus throughout the book of John and defends him as a righteous man to the very end.

Negative Narrative Clues Concerning Nicodemus

It would certainly be too much to suggest that Nicodemus wears a black hat in the text. Yet there are significant clues to indicate that he is an example of what *not* to do when following after Jesus. Some of the clues are subtle but the overall impression is unmistakable.

✝ He comes to Jesus at night. This may simply mean that was when Jesus was available or that was when

Old Men and New Births

40   Nicodemus got off work. However, the kingdom of God *was* Nicodemus's business and Jesus *always* seems to be available for that. No, something deeper is going on here. "Night" and "darkness" occur thirteen times in the book of John (1:5; 3:2,19; 6:17; 8:12; 9:4; 11:10; 12:35,46; 13:30; 19:39; 20:1; 21:3). Nearly every one of these uses is metaphoric—darkness and night symbolize evil, plots, and destruction. For example, when Judas went out to betray Jesus, the author points out "it was night" (11:30). Furthermore, this story begins with night (v. 2) and ends with a description of light vs. darkness (v. 19). In other words, the symbol of darkness surrounds this text. It also seemed an important enough observation for John to mention it twice (cf. 19:39).

† Nicodemus calls Jesus "Rabbi." In light of the fact that he has already been identified in the first two chapters as "Lamb of God," "Son of God," "Messiah," "Logos," and "King of Israel," the mere title "Rabbi" seems a bit myopic. Honorable? Yes. Sufficient? Hardly.

† The conversation begins with Nicodemus being fairly vocal in the first round of the discussion (vv. 1-8). In the second round, however (vv. 9-15), he only asks one question for which he is rebuked because he is so ignorant of things he should understand. In the third round (vv. 16-21) he is completely brushed aside by Jesus' monologue.

† Jesus summarily dismisses all Nicodemus's clout and accomplishments and demands that he start afresh to enter the kingdom. He had to be "born again." There is significant debate whether this indicates immersion or some other spiritual rebirth. That discussion will have to wait for another time. Right here, right now, there is a more important issue. Namely, a person's prestige carries no weight in Jesus' new-world order. The only thing that counts is radical faith in the one who bap-

tizes with the Holy Spirit. The Sanhedrin can't do that.
John the Baptist can't do that. Therefore, if Nicodemus, the Supreme Court Justice, doesn't submit to this peasant carpenter, he has no hopes of an enduring relationship with God.

✝ This leads to one last observation. John 3 really must be read in connection with John 4. There we meet a

Nicodemus	Samaritan Woman
A Jewish Man	A Samaritan Woman
His name was revered	She's given no name
He was morally impeccable	She was a multiple divorcee with a live-in lover
He had financial means	She was without money or even companions
YET	
He comes to Jesus at night	Jesus came to her in the noon-day sun
Jesus demands Nicodemus be reborn in water	Jesus offers her a drink of living water
He confesses Jesus as Rabbi	She proclaims him as Messiah
Nicodemus's colleagues crucify Jesus	The citizens of Sychar, who disrespected her, wound up hailing Jesus as king of the world
Nicodemus never follows Jesus	This woman becomes a model evangelist

woman who is significantly different from Nicodemus.

The lesson seems clear. In the kingdom of God one's clout is irrelevant; one's faith is everything. You can be a good person, a religious, rich, and prestigious person. Jesus cares nothing about that. He cares for a wide-open spirit and a red-

Old Men and New Births

hot heart. So now we revisit our original question: What do we do with a person like Nicodemus? I'm still not sure, but this much I know. Whatever you do, don't imitate him. The closest he ever came to Jesus was his dead body.

Imitating the Person of Jesus

At a church or Christian college or parachurch organization find a conference to attend, that is aimed at sharpening your skills in the areas of either leadership, evangelism, or discipleship. Sign up, go, spend the money needed, take the time off work, pick out helpful resources, be open to change, and then put into practice what you hear and learn.

LIVING WATER FOR A WEARY WOMAN

> "Love talked about can be easily turned aside, but love demonstrated is irresistible."
> —W. Stanley Mooneyham

Text: John 4:1-42   **Memory:** John 4:13-14

Regret When my friend and coworker Shelley, found Granka, she hadn't been cared for in days. Her bed was soaked with urine and sweat and she was, from dehydration, near death. What started out as a simple fever turned deadly because of neglect. Granka would stand among the poorest of the poor in Haiti. Her eyes had seen a lot of injustice and the pain she had endured in life was evident in her face. She was a single mom. Her family was indifferent towards her. They had, in the later stages of her sickness, placed a coffin in her room. Their message to her was quite simple, they weren't hoping she would get well soon. But Shelley fought death. She cleaned Granka up, fed her, and did her best to nurse her back to good health. But her efforts were in vain and Granka died. The morning of her death, I pulled into the compound where our school was located and found my good friend seated at a picnic table, her head in her hands. She had been crying and when I sat down next to her, she did her best to get the words out. Choked up, she said, "I didn't tell her. If I had truly loved her, I would have told her about Jesus."

And when I think about what Shelley said, the words of an old poem come to mind: "Of all sad words of tongue or pen, the saddest are these, 'It might have been.'" When it comes to a few more dollars in an investment, a few more points on a test, or a missed free throw in a basketball game, we can think to ourselves, "it might have been." But when it comes to the eternal, to the kingdom, to restoring and redeeming lost people, what "might have been" just doesn't cut it.

Overview of the Text

Her biography was scandalous; her resume no better. There is absolutely nothing in her cultural background nor in her personal behavior that would commend her to the church. She woke up each morning with a scarlet letter attached to her, but the real terror was the stares and the comments of those around her. Nevertheless, the woman at the well becomes the first great evangelist of the Gospels. Stood next to Nicodemus her story shouts one of the most significant lessons of Christianity. Namely, one's pedigree is of no value in predicting either one's contribution to the kingdom or his relationship with Jesus. In fact, the noonday sun often shines brightest on the outcast. Their effectiveness as evangelists has little to do with their own efforts and much to do with accepting Jesus' bubbling offer of eternal life.

Pondering the Person of Jesus

- Compare and contrast the Samaritan Woman with Nicodemus (you might revisit the notes from the previous lesson). Which of the two are you more like?

✳ Why was it easier for the Samaritan woman to accept Jesus than it was for Nicodemus?

✳ Why do you think Jesus first revealed his Messianic secret to the Samaritan woman?

✳ What does it mean to worship "in Spirit and in Truth"? Do you think it is significant that this new mode of worship is introduced in a context of ethnic evangelism? Explain.

Meaning of the Text   After a 30-mile walk from Judea to Sychar, Jesus sits down at Jacob's well. He had to be pretty pooped. After all, he and the disciples had been walking since sunrise at a pretty good clip. It's now noon and a couple of hours after their normal brunch. The boys run into town to rustle up some grub. Jesus stays for a divine appointment.

Here she came, all by herself (that's telling). She has a jar in her hand and bones in her closet. She is a woman and a Samaritan—that's two strikes against her. Strike one: Women in that day were barely above property . . . in some cases lower. Strike two: Samaritans were enemies of Israel besides being their next-door neighbors. This was a sibling rivalry of sorts. Way back in the days of Solomon, a civil war in Israel split the North from the South. Two hundred years later (c. 722 B.C.), the Assyrians came and displaced the ten northern tribes. They imported other ethnic groups to populate the area and subordinate the land. When they arrived, they began to intermarry with the poor Jews that remained. Thus a new "mulatto" race was born known as Samaritans. The Jews despised them as "half-breeds." The Samaritans retaliated, sometimes with open aggression.

This woman's morals may be questionable, but her intelligence is *not*. She is as sharp as she can be but obviously bested by Jesus. This lady is clearly uncomfortable with the Jewish stranger parked at her well. Her discomfort peaks when he asks for a drink. Their conversation is like a table tennis match with short bursts back and forth. She may think Jesus is just passing the time on a lazy afternoon. He is actually driving deliberately to a critical point that will transform her life. Charted on a graph their repartee looks like this:

Jesus	The Samaritan Woman
Give me a drink.	Why are you talking to me?
If you knew me, you would ask me for living water which I could supply.	Yeah right! You don't even have anything to draw with! Do you think you are greater than Jacob who dug this well?
Actually, yes, I am! After drinking my water you will never thirst again. In fact, I can give you eternal life.	Really?! (Cynical smile). All right pal, I'll take you up on that offer. Show me what you got. Give me some of this water so I don't have to keep coming out here to the well.
Sure, I'll give you some. But first why don't you go get your husband and bring him with you.	I don't have a husband.
How true that is. Yet you've had five already and your present lover is merely a live-in.	Uh . . . So you are a prophet. All right, why don't you answer this question: Are the Jews right to worship exclusively in Jerusalem or are the Samaritans right to worship here on Mt. Gerezim?
Well, actually the Jews are right. But that's soon to be irrelevant because God's children won't worship at a certain place but in Spirit and Truth.	Yeah, whatever. . . . When Messiah comes, he will answer all these thorny theological questions.
Lady, I *AM* the Messiah!	Oh . . .

Just then the disciples return, disconcerted that Jesus was hobnobbing with such riffraff. Yet none of them muster the courage to confront him about it. The woman, meanwhile, runs off, leaving her jar, presumably with the water Jesus asked for in verse 7.

The woman is gone; so is Jesus' appetite. When the disciples offer him food, he says, "I have nourishment you know not of." Have you ever lost your appetite due to excitement? Perhaps it was your first kiss, the sight of a long-lost friend, or a special award you had worked long and hard for. Well, what so excites the Master that he's no longer hungry after a thirty-mile hike? Nothing less than his first open admission of his Messianic mission. He tries to talk about it with the twelve, but they're still pretty thickheaded.

Meanwhile the woman is at work in town. What a brilliant gal! She knows that she doesn't have the clout to draw a crowd so she reverts to cleverness. She finds a group of guys standing around and says, "Come hear a man who told me everything I ever did." Given her reputation, that would be a tantalizing offer. She chases it with a question: "This wouldn't be the Christ, would it?" Now she believes Jesus *is* the Messiah, yet phrases the question so as to expect a negative answer. In other words, she suspects they will disagree with her. Thus she poses the question in such a way that the men can come to a correct conclusion (hers) even while disagreeing with her. (Women can be so savvy!)

Here they come . . . in droves, streaming across the barren fields. Jesus turns to his disciples and says, "Do they not say that there are four months left until the harvest? Well, look up now, the fields are already white unto harvest." The crowd comes to Jesus and becomes convinced that he is, in fact, the Messiah. More than that, they make the most startling declaration to date. They say of Jesus, "He is the savior of the world!"

This is Jesus' greatest revelation of himself so far. This is the greatest confession any disciples make so far. And all

Living Water for a Weary Woman

48 because of a scandalous woman. That's significant, particularly read against the backdrop of Nicodemus in the previous chapter. It introduces us to a key principle of the kingdom—the insiders in this world don't necessarily get front row seats with Jesus. In fact, there is no significant correlation between a person's earthly pedigree and his heavenly status. The deciding factor is faith—faith in Jesus as the one who can make good on his promise of living water. Caution: If you plan to follow Jesus, bring galoshes and an umbrella—he is surrounded by a lot of water.

And speaking of water. Shelley prayed that God would put another woman in her path to share her faith with. And God brought it about in an unbelievable way. Shelley was walking home late one night when she was attacked, beaten to the ground by a young man. He attempted to rape her, but she fought for her life, escaping with bruises and cuts and a dislocated shoulder. She ran down the street screaming and pushed open the first door on the first house that looked open. She collapsed on the floor in shock. And wouldn't you know it, an elderly Haitian woman came to her aide. An elderly woman named Fatalia who didn't know about Jesus. Shelley didn't waste any time this time around. She didn't feel sorry for herself, rather she recognized what God had ordained: a divine appointment with a physically and spiritually impoverished woman. It wasn't long until Shelley walked hand in hand with Fatalia into the waters of the Caribbean. And unlike Granka, who was buried in a public cemetery, Fatalia was buried in the waters of baptism.

Imitating the Person of Jesus

The United States is living up to its title as a "melting pot." Ethnic and cultural diversity can be a positive element in our society if Christians make an effort to tear down walls of prejudice and reach out in love. Make a list

The Person of Jesus

of the different cultural backgrounds represented in the community in which you live. In honest evaluation, what is your church doing to reach the varying people groups? What can be done that isn't being done? Develop a strategy and commit to praying for the "Samaritans" who live among you that don't have a relationship with Jesus.

8   8
HOMETOWN
BOY
THINKS
HE'S A
PROPHET
8   8

> "I think of death
> as a glad awakening
> from this troubled sleep
> that we call life,
> as an emancipation
> from a world, which,
> beautiful though it be,
> is still a land of captivity."
> —Lyman Abbott

Text: Luke 4:14-30   **Memory:** John 1:11

Knocking on Heaven's Door For more than six hundred years the Hapsburgs exercised political power in Europe. When Emperor Franz-Josef I of Austria died in 1916, his was the last of the extravagant imperial funerals. A processional of dignitaries and elegantly dressed court personages escorted the coffin draped in the black-and-gold imperial colors. To the accompaniment of a military band's somber dirges and by the light of torches, the cortege descended the stairs of the Capuchin Monastery of Vienna. At the bottom was a great iron door leading to the Hapsburg family crypt. Behind the door was the Cardinal-Archbishop of Vienna.

The officer in charge followed the prescribed ceremony established centuries before. "Open!" he cried out.

"Who goes there?" responded the Cardinal.

"We bear the remains of his Imperial and Apostolic Majesty, Franz-Josef I, by the grace of God Emperor of Austria, King of Hungary, Defender of the Faith, Prince of Bohemia-Moravia, Grand Duke of Lombardy, Venezia, Styrgia . . . ." The officer continued to list the Emperor's thirty-seven titles.

"We know him not," replied the Cardinal. "Who goes there?"

The officer spoke again, this time using a much abbreviated and less ostentatious title reserved for times of expediency.

"We know him not," the Cardinal said again. "Who goes there?"

The officer tried a third time, stripping the emperor of all but the humblest of titles: "We bear the body of Franz-Josef, our brother, a sinner like us all!"

At that, the doors swung open, and Franz-Josef was admitted.

Sometimes social status is completely worthless in the arena of life. Death is one such event. A person's entrance into the kingdom of God is another example. Though the Jews claimed the inside track to heaven, Jesus promised paradise would be filled with more than the sons of Abraham. Jesus ignored status and said all were eligible for the promise of heaven.

Overview of the Text

Luke alone shares this little vignette. That's a pretty good clue as to its meaning. Often when Luke stands alone, he stands on the ground of *Gentile inclusion*. That is, some stories are particularly interesting to him because they illustrate how outsiders (like him), have been invited in. This is a classic example. He tells us about Jesus' visit to his own hometown. One would expect him to be hailed as a hero. Yet he is nearly assassinated. Why the sudden burst of aggression? Because Jesus applied Messianic prophecy to himself even

Hometown Boy Thinks He's a Prophet

from the pulpit of his hometown synagogue. What's worse, when they called him on it, he had the audacity to suggest that these insiders were out while outsiders were getting in. Luke likes that. Let's see how you feel about it.

Pondering the Person of Jesus

✕ What kind of people would cause raised eyebrows at your church?

✕ Be honest; in what ways do you feel that you are an insider at the church? What characteristics or activities make someone an "insider"?

✕ What practical steps could we take to help our church become more inclusive?

✕ What other stories in the Gospels or Acts illustrate how inclusive the gospel is?

Meaning of the Text

Going home . . . what an experience. It is often a strange blend of nostalgia, celebration, and frustration. We like to remember our childhood; we dislike being treated as a child. Uncles and parents, siblings and next-door neighbors have a knack for recalling our most awkward moments of puberty. Our flaws seem magnified through the lens of reminiscence. Our ordinariness overshadows our adult accomplishments.

Imagine what it was like for Jesus. He has been immersed into ministry and tempted by the Devil. He has gathered his first followers, cleansed the temple, and turned water into wine. His reputation as a preacher and wonder-worker is spreading more quickly than tabloid gossip. Everywhere everyone is fascinated with him. This is the kind of thing that makes a small town proud of its local hero. Yet when he comes home, folks feel obligated to whittle him down to provincial size. "Sure he's great," they say, "He just needs to remember where he came from. We can't have the fella getting too big for his tunic."

The story unfolds with the scroll in the synagogue. Jesus was asked to address the congregation that raised him in that sacred precinct. The synagogue leader hands him the scroll. He solemnly turns the large wooden handles until he locates Isaiah 61. There he reads the first two verses (leaving off the second half of verse 2—that would be a sermon for another day). He chose well. It was a familiar and beloved passage. All eyes were on him waiting to hear what he would say about this text. "Today this scripture is fulfilled in your hearing. That's right, folks, Isaiah was talking about me." Their ears perked up; their eyes bugged out. An audible rumble makes its way across the auditorium.

His claim was bodacious; his words, eloquent. The locals don't know what to do with this. They can believe that one of their own would become famous. They have difficulty, however, imagining that he would be the liberator of the nation. After all, he was the son of a carpenter, just an ordinary Joe(seph). In those days there was virtually no movement between classes. It was much like the caste system in India. His dad (in actuality his stepfather), was a blue-collar worker in a small rural village. It just doesn't make sense to them that this boy they watched grow up would have the right stuff to lead a nation. Little do they know. . . .

Jesus is sharp. He perceives exactly what they are thinking and condenses it to a proverb, "Physician, heal yourself." He had been doing spectacular miracles that won him attention in Capernaum. "If he would only do such things here, we would believe in him," they think to themselves. Jesus knows better. He counters with another proverb, "No prophet is accepted in his hometown." In other words, it doesn't matter what Jesus does here, they aren't going to believe him. This is true. Preachers often have more credibility away from home. It's the same with actors, politicians, and scientists as well. There is something about anonymity that increases one's credibility.

Hometown Boy Thinks He's a Prophet

54   In Jesus' case, however, there is something deeper going on. It is not merely that his own village will reject him; so will Galilee. Capernaum, for example, where he did so many of his miracles, wound up walking away (cf. Matt. 11:23). Broader still, the entire nation, epitomized by the city of Jerusalem, rejected and assassinated him (cf. John 1:11). This text is bigger than a village. It's bigger than a region. It encompasses an entire nation. Jesus' own people rejected him. Therefore, his offer of salvation broke through the ethnic barriers of Palestine and extended to outsiders. As Paul says, "I am not ashamed of the gospel, because it is the power of God for the salvation of everyone who believes: first for the Jew, then for the Gentile" (Rom. 1:16). This would become a pattern of evangelism in the book of Acts. In every city with a synagogue Paul first preached to Jews. After they rejected the message and/or persecuted the preacher, he ran off to the Gentiles who often gladly received the offer of salvation.

It may look like Jesus is bogus because those who knew him best rejected him. However, this is merely evidence that he stands in elite company. The most prominent prophets experienced the same thing. Jesus calls two to mind: Elijah and Elisha. Both preached in Israel. Both were rejected. Both broke the boundaries by ministering to Gentiles. Elijah raised the widow's son and Elisha cleansed Naaman from leprosy. Yet when Jesus does the same thing, he is faced with the same contempt as they.

There was nothing false about what Jesus said, just irritating. In fact, his words make them so mad they tried to kill him. They usher him right out to the edge of a cliff to chuck him off the edge. But Jesus "walked right through the crowd and went on his way." This is one of those curious Bible events that make you wish you were there. Did Jesus walk along willingly until he got to the edge? Did he use miraculous power to blind their eyes when he walked away? Or did he

turn with righteous indignation and back them off with a
glare? Our imaginations are pricked at such a curious scene.

This much we know, however. This is the first attempt on Jesus' life, and it comes from those who should have been his staunchest supporters. Furthermore, the issue that irked them was the idea that the Messiah's ministry would break the boundaries of Israel. They no longer had exclusive rights to the heart of God. It somehow made them feel less special, indeed threatened. Jesus disavowed their private ownership of God. Imagine the audacity! And when he did, we were all stripped of titles, positions, and nationalities. We've been grouped together as sinners, but the door to heaven has been opened for us all!

Imitating the Person of Jesus

Fill in the following chart.

	Attempt on Jesus' Life	Reason They Tried to Kill Him	Result
Luke 4:29			
John 7:30			
John 8:59			
John 10:31			
John 10:39			

Analyze why Jesus' enemies tried to get rid of him. Given these reasons, what kind of reception do you think Jesus might receive at your church? Avoid gossip, but describe specifically the kinds of obstacles he might run into.

Hometown Boy Thinks He's a Prophet

9 9
FUTURE FISHERS OF MEN
9 9

> "Must one point out
> that from ancient times
> a decline in courage
> has been considered
> the beginning of the end?"
> —Aleksandr Solzhenitsyn

Text: Luke 5:1-11   **Memory:** Luke 5:10b-11

Courage   A federal judge had ordered New Orleans to open its public schools to African-American children. White parents in the community decided to keep their children at home if this verdict was enforced. They made it known that any African-American children who came to school would suffer the consequences. So the black children, in fear, stayed home too.

That is, everyone except Ruby Bridges. Her parents sent her to school all by herself, six years old. Every morning she walked alone through a heckling crowd to an empty school. White people lined up on both sides of the way and shook their fists at her. They threatened to do terrible things to her if she kept coming to their school. But every morning at ten minutes to eight Ruby walked, head up, eyes ahead, straight through the mob; two U.S. marshals walked ahead of her and two walked behind her. Then she spent the day alone with her teachers inside that big silent school building.

Harvard professor Robert Coles was curious about what went into the making of courageous children like Ruby Bridges. He talked to Ruby's mother and, in his book *The Moral Life of Children,* tells what she said: "There's a lot of people who talk about doing good, and a lot of people who argue about what's good and what's not good," but there are other folks who "just put their lives on the line for what's right."

Knowing the difference between right and wrong is part of the battle our culture is fighting, but taking the next step is a scary one. It involves courage. The kind of courage that changes lives.

Overview of the Text

These four fishermen had followed Jesus for more than a year. They had listened to him preach, seen him heal people, gasped when he cleansed the temple, and laughed out loud when he turned water into wine. They think they know him . . . they haven't a clue. What they are about to experience will stretch their faith; it will demolish their presuppositions. When they see Jesus control the forces of nature in their own back yard, it will make them so uncomfortable they will ask him to leave. It is at this very place of discomfort and confusion that their relationship with Jesus will come into its clearest focus. When they see him for who he really is, they will understand they cannot be passive followers but must become full-time fishers of men. So it is with us. A clear vision of Jesus often turns our comfortable existence into turbulence. Yet it brings into focus our obligation to unmitigated devotion to the master.

Pondering the Person of Jesus

- What people, experiences, or things prevent you from truly abandoning it all to follow Jesus?
- What is the most courageous thing you've ever done for Jesus?

Future Fishers of Men

✳ If you feared nothing but God, what do you think
you would like to try to do for the gospel?

✳ What would be the hardest person, possession, and
occupation for you to give up if Jesus asked you to
do so?

Meaning of the Text

When Jesus' tour finally returns to Capernaum, it only makes sense that the fishermen would resume business. There would be bills to pay and families to support. Unfortunately the fish are uncooperative. They lay low all night, giving the fishermen fits. Normally the north shore of the lake is lucrative but not this time. They get skunked. You know how surly fishermen can be when their luck runs dry. It's worse when you're trying to make a living rather than out for sport. They are tired, frustrated, and struggling to make ends meet.

That may not be the best time for Jesus to show up, but there he was. In fact, he asked Peter to use his boat as a pulpit. He was so wildly popular that the crowds pressed him right to the water's edge. The boat allowed Jesus to use the shore as a natural amphitheater. The multitudes were mesmerized. (Actually, we don't know what Jesus said, but his other sermons were usually pretty good.)

When he finished, he told Peter to row out into the deep water and let down his nets. What a bummer! You see, Peter knew the best fishing was already over. Furthermore, they had just finished cleaning the nets. Obeying Jesus can often be a real hassle! I don't know what Peter was thinking, or muttering under his breath, as he obeyed. Perhaps it was something like: "You may be an excellent carpenter and a famous preacher, but you really should leave the fishing to me!" All of a sudden the tension on the other end of the net told Peter he had something significant. His muscles bulged, his eyes bugged out. As fistfuls of net cascaded over the side of the boat, he realized this was a bigger blessing than he bargained for.

The Person of Jesus

His Cheshire smile turned to a grimace as he realized he needed more help. Luke says they "signaled their partners." The word he uses indicates "to nod with the head." That makes sense since Peter can't very well let go to wave at them. James and John hustle out with the other boat. Placing the net between the two boats they begin to haul in the catch. Fish are flopping over into the boat. They begin to squirm in massive piles which drive the boat deeper into the water. They keep pulling; the fish keep coming. Soon they realize they are in danger of sinking due to the massive catch.

When all is said and done, the boat creeps back to shore laden with a blessing. In one fell swoop Jesus eradicated nine months of sacrifice. At this point Peter does the strangest thing. He falls on his knees in a squirming pile of mackerel and says, "Lord, depart from me, for I am a sinful man." One might think Peter would want Jesus around. After all, he's good for business. It was a wonderful and exciting day. Surely folks on the shore enjoyed this immensely. Perhaps they even sold "I was at the great catch" T-shirts.

Why on earth would Peter petition Jesus to leave him alone? Answer: Because Peter was in the boat. He made his living on this volatile lake. He knew its power. Jesus came to Peter's turf and governed the forces of nature. This rough-and-tumble fisherman is faced with the reality that his running buddy is far more majestic than a mere magician with a few tricks up his sleeve. He is more powerful than a prophetic preacher who wows the crowd with some revolutionary dialogue. This man stands where Yahweh alone has heretofore trod. Peter is right to fear him just as Isaiah did when he met him (Isa. 6:1; John 12:41). There is a battle being waged for authenticity. Peter is the imperfect one standing in the perfect presence of Jesus. Like Quasimodo, that beloved character from *The Hunchback of Notre Dame*, he has become comfortable in his place of hiding. "Why give people a chance to see the

Future Fishers of Men

real me? That person scarred and disfigured by sin?" So Peter hides. Not in the belfry of a cathedral but behind the guise of a net and oars and sails. But like little kids who play hide-and-seek, we want to be found. We snap branches and whistle and giggle, hoping the one who is "it" will chase after us.

Jesus does chase after Peter and demands that Peter do the same. He says, "No, I won't leave you. Furthermore, you won't leave me. You will continue to follow me, and I will show you how to fish for men." Luke uses a wonderful word for "catch men" (v. 10). It means "to take live captives" (2 Tim. 2:26). As Jesus walked along he called the others in the same way. Peter, Andrew, James, and John now have a new occupation. They are full-time followers of Jesus and future leaders in this great evangelistic enterprise. They have known and loved Jesus for over a year. It is now time to step it up to a new level of faith and commitment.

What about you? Have you ever been in the boat? Has Jesus ever come to your turf and demonstrated extraordinary power? Perhaps you thought you really knew who he was until he suddenly pulled back the curtain. Then his identity overwhelmed you like a tsunami of deity. What do you do then? What will you do now? Hiding is futile. Once he has shown his face, he refuses to leave you alone. He neither slips gently away nor does he allow you to do the same. He is demanding and relentless and passionate in his pursuit. There are other fish to catch. Now that you've heard the call, what will your next move be? Will you courageously take a stand for what is right? Will you be the one who walks through the crowds, head up, eyes fixed on the one you've been called to follow?

1. Write a letter to a person in your small group or church family. Thank her for the example she has been to you during your spiritual development.
2. Write another letter to a person, encouraging him to continue his pursuit of Jesus and challenging him to use his God-given gifts.

10 OUT 10 WITH THE OLD, IN WITH THE GOOD NEWS

10 10

> "Spiritual pride is the main door by which the devil comes into the hearts of those who are zealous for the advancement of truth. It is the chief inlet of smoke from the bottomless pit to darken the mind and mislead the judgment."
> —Jonathan Edwards

> "We are not converted to be introverted."
> —Richard H. Seume

Text: Matthew 9:9-17   **Memory:** Matthew 9:12-13

Unaware   A Los Angeles County parking control officer came upon a brown El Dorado Cadillac illegally parked next to the curb on street-sweeping day. The officer dutifully wrote out a ticket. Ignoring the man seated at the driver's wheel, the officer reached inside the open car window and placed the $30 citation on the dashboard.

The driver of the car made no excuses. No arguments ensued—and with good reason. The driver of the car had been shot in the head ten to twelve hours before but was sitting up, stiff as a board, slumped slightly forward, with blood on his face. He was dead. The officer, preoccupied with ticket writing, was unaware of anything out of the ordinary. He got back in his car and drove away.

Many people around us are dead in their sins. What should catch our attention most is their need, not their offenses. They don't need a citation; they need a Savior. And I think it safe to say that Matthew was on the receiving end of some stares and finger pointing and name calling and ticket writing when Jesus came his way.

Overview of the Text

Some things are clearly inappropriate: Giggling at a funeral, hitting on a woman in a wedding dress, chewing tobacco in a dentist's office. This text introduces us to a couple of other things that just don't fit: (1) Fasting while Jesus is with you, and (2) keeping sick people from the Great Physician. Both points stand on the shoulders of a man named Matthew. He is not well liked because he works for the Roman IRS, extorting taxes from the poor of his own people. His personal success comes at the great cost of social rejection. Against all odds, Jesus calls Matthew to follow him. Then the fireworks fly.

Pondering the Person of Jesus

- What public figure can you think of who needs to have a relationship with Jesus?
- What friend or family member have you written off as a "lost cause" because of his sinful lifestyle?
- What types of people are the hardest for you to evangelize? Do you think your biggest difficulty in evangelism is fear or prejudice?
- Have each person in the group tell of his own conversion and then vote on who is most like Matthew.

Meaning of the Text

Have you ever walked into a room and just groaned? You look across the crowd and there s/he is—that person who makes your skin crawl. Well, then you know how Peter feels right now. It is one of those days when Jesus is teaching, the crowds are growing, and Peter is right in the thick of the action. Things are going *so* well—until they get to the booth. Oh, Peter knew that dreaded booth. That's where Levi sat day after day. He was one of those slimy turncoats who collected taxes from Abraham's children and fed it to the pagans of Rome. In fact, because Peter fished this north shore of the lake, he had been stuck time and again dishing out dole to Levi's coffers. The bigger his catch the worse Levi robbed him. Peter just seethes with anger.

Suddenly Jesus stops, right in front of the IRS office. That was a mistake, and Peter knew it. Here is where he instinctively picks up the pace and tries to sneak by. I imagine Simon is a few steps gone before he realizes he's lost his escort. He turns to see Jesus staring down the enemy. Perhaps it is one of those slow motion moments for Peter as he hears Jesus say those immortal words, "Folloooooooow Meeee." "No, not him Lord! Don't you know who you're talking to? He'll ruin the party." Turns out, however, he's the one throwing the party. But this must wait.

Here Matthew sits in his pinstriped tunic. Jesus makes a radical demand. Matthew obeys. This is impressive at a couple of levels. First, Matthew is not the only one Jesus ever called vocationally, yet none, to date, have sacrificed so much. You see, when the fishermen follow Jesus, they leave their boat in the hands of their family and servants who can carry on the business. They will always have their nets to fall back on. Matthew is different. Once he leaves the booth, there is a line of loan sharks eager to take his spot. If he leaves now, it is for good; if he follows Jesus, it must be forever.

Second, Matthew was an unlikely convert. He was surrounded by other publicans, despised by the Hebrews. Because of his job he was not allowed into the synagogue. He was considered a filthy traitor. On the one hand, he is shunned; on the other, he is surrounded by materialistic and hedonistic pleasures. What would a guy like that do with Jesus? Answer: Like everyone else, he would bow before the

The Person of Jesus

master and find in him the satisfaction of his soul. In fact, of all the Gospels, Matthew quotes more Old Testament Scripture than anyone. Apparently he had deep longings that were invisible on the surface. More than that, he had a deep love for the very people who had shunned him. For it is he who strives to reach them through his writings.

In March of 1995, the New England Pipe Cleaning Company of Watertown, Connecticut, was digging twenty-five feet beneath the streets of Revere, Massachusetts, in order to clean a clogged 10-inch sewer line.

In addition to the usual materials one might expect to find in a clogged sewer line, the three-man team found 61 rings, vintage coins, eyeglasses, and silverware, all of which they were allowed to keep.

Whether it's pipes or people, if you put up with some mess, sometimes you find real treasure. And, there are many who appear to be antagonistic to the things of God. Yet their deep longings, hidden beneath a crusty surface, cry out to follow Jesus. Given half a chance and a clear call, they are off and running. Don't write them off just because they've succeeded in the flesh. Even hedonistic materialism can't quiet the voice that clamors for the peace of God.

Matthew is so excited that he simply must share his new-found friend with his old running buddies. So he throws a party. All his colleagues show up. What a motley crew. The place was packed with loan sharks and lawyers and the kind of women they date. To the Kosher in the crowd it could only be described as "icky." They begin to grumble: "Birds of a feather flock together." They go so far as to corner Jesus' disciples and ask, "What kind of a person is Jesus? Why are all his best friends such sinners?" Now that was a low blow. The Pharisees' clout fell heavy on these blue-collar types. Their education and religious authority intimidated them. And

Out with the Old, In with the Good News

frankly, they were a bit baffled by Jesus right now as well. You see, they operated under the same presupposition: Religious people avoid sinners.

Jesus comes to the rescue. He also changes the paradigm. We no longer operate under "Birds of a feather . . ." but "The sick need a physician." Jesus came to seek and to save the lost. Therefore it was precisely a guy like Matthew who needed him. It is difficult to overstate the importance of this new paradigm. It is also difficult to overestimate how few churches have adopted it. There is no written creed that commands sinners to clean up their act before coming to Christ. Nonetheless, our unwritten rules are very clear. Our body language and ecclesiastical ambience shouts: "You better wipe your feet before coming into our church!" Just try lighting a cigarette in the foyer or letting a little "French" fly across a pew and see how quickly the morality police appear. Try bringing a friend to church with piercings or dying a stripe down the side of your head. Confess a sin from the pulpit and see how deathly quiet the congregation gets. Now, it is not that Jesus is against moral behavior. Nonetheless, he is violently opposed to making it a prerequisite to a relationship. He loved lost people, not because of their lifestyles but because of their potential to become trophies of grace.

You see, we operate under the old paradigm that the church is a place for somber saints rather than jubilant sinners. Jesus objected. "This is a party!" He protested. "A lost person has been found. How dare you fast when there's a feast to be had!" Such sadness is inappropriate in the presence of the Author of Life. It is as awkward as a new patch on an old pair of pants that tears when it is washed. It is as destructive as new wine in an old wineskin that bursts as it ferments.

We have a new message that doesn't fit the old ecclesiastical paradigm. We no longer look somber in the presence of God. We no longer prize ascetic purity or isolation from sinners. Jesus inaugurates a new day dawning. He has come and so has life incarnate. We have good news for sinners and an invitation from home going out to all prodigals. Perhaps all the king's horses and all of his men couldn't put Humpty Dumpty back together again. But Jesus can. . . . He did. . . . He will.

Imitating the Person of Jesus

Interview someone who has recently been converted. Ask them three questions:

1) What difference has Jesus made in your life?
2) What was the hardest thing about attending church?
3) Describe your best friends. How have they responded to your conversion?

11 11
A LAME
LOSER
AND A
PLATFORM
FOR
PREACHING
11 11

> "Life with Christ is an endless hope,
> without Him a hopeless end."
> —Anonymous

Text: John 5:1-47   **Memory:** John 5:24

Cleanliness Next to Godliness

The American Society for Microbiology recently studied the handwashing habits of Americans and found some disturbing results. According to the Associated Press, the researchers hid in stalls or pretended to comb their hair as they observed 6,333 men and women in restrooms in five major cities.

The results: In New York's Penn Station only 60 percent of those using the restrooms washed up. At a Braves game in Atlanta a mere 64 percent washed their hands. For a germ-fearing, soap-toting society, those are hypocritical statistics.

"Hand washing in this country has become all but a lost art," said Dr. Michael Osterholm, a Minnesota state epidemiologist. The Center for Disease Control and Prevention says that hand washing is one of the "most important means of preventing the spread of infection."

God also has advice on how to be clean—that is, how to be clean within—for our spiritual health likewise depends on it. We can only come clean through the power and person of Jesus Christ.

Overview of the Text

This is a very strange miracle. Jesus walks into a "sick ward" and heals only one person. This scalawag has neither faith nor integrity. So why would Jesus heal *him*? Every other miracle Jesus performed was prompted either by compassion or apologetics. In other words, Jesus isn't being "nice" to the guy, nor is he proving his power. He is throwing down the gauntlet. He heals this imp to start a fight. It was fierce too. (By the way, Jesus won). The surface issue is the Sabbath. Don't get distracted by that, however. The real issue is Jesus' identity. Lift your gaze from the law, and fix your eyes on Jesus. He is the center of this story. In this text you will have the unprecedented opportunity to listen to Jesus talk about himself. You might not believe what he says, but you will hear him tell you precisely who *he* thinks he is.

Pondering the Person of Jesus

✳ When is it right to pick a fight? Why does Jesus do so here?

✳ Why was it so difficult for Jesus' listeners to see his true identity?

✳ Describe clearly who you think Jesus is.

✳ What is so dangerous about the praise of men (vv. 41-44)?

Meaning of the Text

I've never liked this guy and you can't make me. Oh sure, I feel sorry for him (after all, he's an invalid). But not all physically challenged people are necessarily nice. In fact, some of them are downright surly. Jesus meets him by the Pool of Bethesda. Now there's an interesting place. It was surrounded by five

A Lame Loser and a Platform for Preaching

70 porches and was apparently fed by a spring that bubbled intermittently. According to the local lore, the first sick person to dive in after the waters bubbled got healed. There's a fine how-do-ya-do. The person who needs it least is most likely to get better. Those with hangnails or bunions were the first to do a cannon ball into the pool. I'm certain that a good number of the invalids lying there actually believed they would be healed. Nonetheless, this doesn't sound like God's M.O. After all, that would be kind of a mean trick to help the least helpless.

Back to the text. Jesus saunters up to this man who had been paralyzed for 38 years. He asks, "Do you want to get well?" The obvious answer is, "Yes!!!" But that's not what he says. Rather he complains about having no friends to pitch him into the pool when it bubbles. Really?! No friends . . . . Could it be that he has become comfortable feeding off of the sympathy of others? Jesus cuts to the chase and orders him on his way. The man obeys. Notice, however, there's no fanfare. This episode lacks the normal talk about rejoicing, praising God, and worshiping Jesus. That's significant.

The man doesn't get far before he is accosted by the religious leaders. You see, it is Saturday and he is carrying his mat. They had rules against such things. When questioned, he immediately passes the buck: "It's not my fault, that guy that healed me made me do it!" When they ask him who healed him, he doesn't know. Apparently he is so self-absorbed that he didn't bother to even find out Jesus' name.

Later they meet again in the temple. Jesus has some not-so-gentle words for him. "Stop sinning or something worse may happen to you." This threat plays off a common Jewish belief. That is, many in those days thought that physical ailments were a result of a person's sin. (While that is sometimes true, they applied it unilaterally). In this instance, however, the something worse is not being a quadriplegic rather

than a paraplegic. Jesus' isn't threatening to break both his
arms and legs if he doesn't straighten up. Rather, Jesus is
threatening him with hell. This man was touched by the
Master, yet his heart remained unchanged. That's dangerous
in the extreme.

You would think this guy would quiver in reverence after that.
But, no, he runs off to the authorities and finks. "Hey, you
asked who healed me. It was that guy over there. They call
him Jesus. Yeah, he's the one you're looking for." You know
what makes this most offensive? This man has been paralyzed for 38 years. That means he has not been in the temple
for that whole time because those with physical deformities
were not allowed in according to Mosaic law. Furthermore, he
would not have entered the temple the first twelve years of his
life. Thus, unless he is more than fifty, this is his first trip to
the sacred precincts. Given the limited life-span of the desti-
tute, it is highly unlikely that he is that old. Therefore, we can
suggest with some degree of certainty that he has never
entered this place before. He must be gawking with wide-
eyed wonder. This had to have been an overpowering religious experience for him. He is faced with a choice—loyalty
to Jesus or to the religious hierarchy. The pressure to cower
to the latter should not be underestimated. Nonetheless, his
healing by Jesus was the very thing that allowed him in the
temple in the first place. He should have known better. He
does not choose wisely. He rejects the true temple in favor of
a cheap substitute. The one who gained him access is excised
from his life. Oh, don't hate him completely. He doesn't stand
alone—nor so far away.
    Now that the leaders have ammunition against the
Master, they waste no time using it. They aren't taking mild
potshots either. This is a full-scale assault. Verse 18 is key,
"The Jews tried all the harder to kill him." They consider him
such a threat that they feel justified in breaking the sixth

A Lame Loser and a Platform for Preaching

commandment. Again, the real issue isn't Sabbath keeping. That was merely the smoke screen. The real issue is Jesus' identity. He was claiming Yahweh as his father. The Jews truly believe "like father, like son." Thus what Jesus says sounds like blasphemy.

In their minds Jesus was an arrogant, heretical megalomaniac whose blasphemous claims deserved death. He was increasingly popular and thus had to be exterminated, not just isolated or rebuffed. Jesus' healing was a success. It accomplished its desired goal by throwing the cards on the table face up. This present hand will need to be dealt with.

The Master responds to their frontal assault with a volley of his own. This sermon (vv. 19-47) is the clearest declaration to date of his person and purpose. He pulls no punches and minces no words. In fact, it is so forthright that even many Christians balk at its clarity and consequence. Here he claims to be God's envoy with all its rights and privileges. In fact, he's not only a servant come to save, he is coming again to judge. And judge he will, without preference or wavering, he will send to hell all those who reject him. This issue is not merely morality, but identity. Those who cling to Christ will find life, resurrection, and reward. Those who reject him head into eternity damned. Thus the lame man serves as a paradigm for potential disciples. All of us must face Christ and determine if his claims are valid.

These are outrageous assertions for one who wears skin. Thus, according to Moses' jurisprudence, Jesus justifies his claims by multiple witnesses. John the Baptist, the Scriptures, Moses, even Yahweh, stand beside Jesus to verify the truth of his claims. Jesus could, of course, be lying, or downright deceived. Are those possibilities? Nevertheless, the claims themselves are so consequential that they dare not be ignored. One last witness is the legacy he leaves behind: the saved and transformed life. Your name and my name were

The Person of Jesus

etched into the grain of a bloodstained cross. We had better decide which side we're on. The stakes are greater than life and death.

Imitating the Person of Jesus

1. Read aloud three passages in John: verses 19-23, then 24-30, then 31-47. After each section, stop and make a list of Jesus' credentials.
2. Develop a resume for Jesus under these three headings:
   1) *Background* (Jesus' relationship to God)
   2) *Job Description*
   3) *References* (people who testified about Jesus)
3. Sometime this week, based on this resume, write out on a single piece of paper, just what you believe about Jesus.
4. Pretend you are a lawyer and Jesus' deity is on trial. Make a list of the "evidence" you would introduce to the court to prove his claims.

A Lame Loser and a Platform for Preaching

12   12

A NEW VIEW OF SATURDAY

12   12

Text: Matthew 12:1-11   **Memory:** Matthew 12:12

Virus of False Teaching

John Norstad, a Northwestern University systems engineer and computer guru who invented "Disinfect," a software program that protects computers from viruses, once discovered the source of many computer viruses. In an interview with writer Peter Gorner, Norstad said: "I went to a conference in Europe and met most of my counterparts in the PC antiviral community. One fellow consultant and designer was a Bulgarian who told us about the Bulgarian virus-writing factory.

"Evidently, during the Communist heyday of the 1980s, the KGB trained and paid PC programmers to break Western copy-protection schemes. It was an official piracy program meant to frustrate computer users on a global scale. Then when the government fell in Bulgaria, all these people were out of work and bitter. So they formed virus-writing clubs and

set about infecting the PC community worldwide. A significant percentage of the PC viruses came out of a group of disenfranchised hackers who had formerly worked for the
Communists."

Computer viruses are a lot like false teachings about
God and morality: they destroy what is valuable.

Pondering the Person of Jesus

✗ In what way does Jesus bring rest into your life?
   What area of your life is needlessly wearing you
   out?

✗ If a visitor came into your church, what kind of
   things would they think were important to you?
   What kind of things might they identify as "idols"?

✗ What sorts of issues in your church are being cham-
   pioned as gospel when in fact they are simply good
   moral principles? How has this affected your
   church's outreach?

Meaning of the Text

Every church has its idols. You
know, those golden calves. In
ancient days they were made of wood and stone. Today they
are a bit more amorphous. Sometimes they look like sched-
ules or programs. At other times they take shape as rituals or
buildings. But you can always tell when you smash one by
the reaction of the crowd. These icons are never intended to
replace God, but sometimes they inadvertently do. We protect them tenaciously because so often we find our identity in
them rather than the person of Christ. It could be our organ
music or raised hands, our version of the Bible or our minister's charisma. We identify ourselves by our pet idols.

They may not make much sense to outsiders or even to
us. But they must be carefully guarded because these are the
things that separate us from the riffraff that try to imitate true
Christians. For instance, some churches get their identity by

A New View of Saturday

the style of their music or their rejection of certain instruments. Others make their mark with certain doctrines or social work. These aren't bad, in and of themselves, until they distract us from the person of Christ. At that point we are likely to find Jesus viciously iconoclastic.

In Oliver Cromwell's day the British government ran out of silver for coins. Cromwell sent his men to the cathedral to see if they could find any there. They returned and reported, "The only silver we can find is in the statues of the saints standing in the corners." To which the great soldier and statesman of England replied, "Good. We'll melt down the saints and put them in circulation!" It may be time to do the same.

In Jesus' day, the Jews had their own icons. One of them was the Sabbath. What's odd is that Sabbath was given by God yet still transformed into an idol. Along with a kosher diet and peculiar dress, these were how Jews marked themselves before the watching world. The sacred Sabbath thus became a sacred cow. As a result, they adorned it with all kinds of rules. In fact, in the Talmud, there is an entire chapter devoted to nothing but rules of what one could and could not do on the Sabbath. Some get pretty persnickety. For instance, if a chicken lays an egg on the Sabbath, you cannot eat that egg because it was the product of work. However, you could hatch the egg that was laid on the Sabbath and later eat that chicken. Or you could hatch the egg that was laid on the Sabbath and allow that chicken to lay eggs and then eat the eggs that were laid by the chicken that was hatched from the egg that was laid on the Sabbath (so long as those eggs were not laid on the Sabbath). It gets so ludicrous it's comical. There were rules about carrying weight, latching your sandals, looking in a mirror, and lighting candles. In walks Jesus. His vision is clear. There is going to be a confrontation.

One Saturday, Jesus and the boys are walking through a grain field. They get hungry so they snag a snack. If you've

The Person of Jesus

ever done it, you know how delightful it is. You grab a few 77
heads of wheat, roll them in your hand, puff real hard and
voila, all that's left is the tasty little grains. The farmers back
then actually expected you to do that. In fact, the law com-
manded that the corners and edges of the field be reserved for
pilgrims (Deut. 23:25). So the problem for the Pharisees was
not trespassing or theft. It was a breach of Sabbath etiquette.
According to Pharisaic rules, the disciples had worked in
three different ways. They harvested by plucking the grain,
threshed by rubbing the grain, and winnowed by blowing on
it. Now you might think Jesus would simply say, "Come on,
guys, that's microscopic stupidity!" But Jesus' intention is not
merely that they correctly interpret the rules, but that they
see clearly his person. Watch.

Jesus justifies his students with two examples: David and the
Priests. David violated the written law in 1 Samuel 21:1-6
when he ate the "consecrated bread" as he was fleeing from
Saul. Likewise, the Priests break the Sabbath by necessity
when they serve in the Temple. They butcher animals for the
sacrifices, yet they are not guilty of breaking the Sabbath.
Now, if David and the priests can justifiably ignore the written law in service to God, how much more can Jesus' disciples justifiably ignore the oral traditions of the Pharisees in
service of Jesus?! You see, the oral traditions were less than
the law, and Jesus is greater than both David and the priests.

The point here, however, is not merely justification of
Jesus' disciples. The point is the identification of Jesus. He
claims to be greater than king David and even greater than
the temple itself. (Feathers are going to fly!) In fact, Jesus ful-
fills all the hopes, dreams, and institutions of Judaism. He is
the temple raised in three days. He is the new Moses, lawgiv-
er, and liberator. He is David, the king. He is the Passover and
the mercy seat. He is even Sabbath itself—the very rest we
need. The point is this: The disciples are with Jesus. When

A New View of Saturday

they serve him, they are, by default, keeping Sabbath and need not meticulously follow man-made regulations. Did you register that?! Jesus is the Sabbath. Therefore, when you are with him, you *are* keeping the Sabbath!

The next story takes us to a synagogue. A man was there with a withered limb; according to Jerome it was crushed in a masonry accident. It's hard to tell, but it looks as if he has been planted there to see what Jesus would do. You see, it was illegal to heal on the Sabbath. At least that's what the Pharisees said. God apparently disagreed.

Jesus asks a simple question, "Which is lawful on the Sabbath: to do good or to do evil, to save life or to kill?" The answer seems obvious, but no one says a word. Undoubtedly they wanted to say, "Neither!" After all, if this guy really was a mason, then he can't work until the next day anyway. Thus Jesus' healing, according to the Pharisees, didn't do the man any immediate good, and it violated their rules. But for Jesus, to refrain from doing good when one has the chance is tantamount to doing evil. Think about how true that is. When we neglect to do good in order to satisfy a religious requirement, we have replaced the best with the good and created an idol enshrined to ourselves. Our postponement of mercy in lieu of religious ritual betrays a self-aggrandizement that is truly culpable. Such a person is warped to the core. Any good deeds s/he does perform are merely a thin façade plastered on the surface of a vile interior.

Jesus, predictably, heals the man, who is as delighted as the Pharisees are infuriated. How dare Jesus insubordinately defy their authority right in front of them! You know what? They aren't the only ones mad right now. Jesus too is irate. That's uncommon. In fact, there were only two other times that the Gospels point out Jesus' ire (John 2:15-17 and Mark 10:14). Here he is angry because religious ritual superseded human need. In itself, that is a bad thing. But it gets worse see, the purpose of the Sabbath is to foster a relationship with God. The first episode demonstrates how far afield they were from knowing who Jesus really was. This second episode is merely another nail in that same coffin. If they knew God, they would know Jesus. Not only would they know Jesus, they would love people. Here, however, they are using a crippled man to catch Jesus doing good and thus convict him of being evil. It is truly twisted, but not completely unfamiliar. We too are often guilty of following religious rules away from the person of Christ.

How often does our dress keep others out of church or our religious vocabulary intimidate the outcast? How often do we worship at the altar of conservativism rather than show liberal love? How often do our pulpits ring with vicious attacks on alcohol, tobacco, and movies that can hardly be justified by a single book/chapter/verse? We must be careful that our own evangelical regulations don't become idols that cloud a clear vision of the person of Christ. He is our Saturday. In him is rest, freedom, nourishment, and healing. That is a sign the world needs to see hanging in every church entrance. If we miss that, we had better check our phylacteries at the door.

Imitating the Person of Jesus

Invite a non-Christian friend to anonymously attend your church. Share with him/her this lesson and tell him/her you want his/her help to identify those "signs" your church puts up.

A New View of Saturday

13 THE ROCK ON WHICH WE STAND

13   13   13   13

Text: Matthew 16:13-23   **Memory:** Matthew 16:15-16

Life and Death

The infamous predictor of days gone by, Nostradamus, stumbled across an elderly woman in northern France during the time of a great plague. The woman, near death, was lying on a street where many other dead bodies were located. Most of the people in the small town had succumbed to the atrocious and indiscriminate plague. Fearing that no one would be left to give her a proper burial when she died, the woman decided to take matters into her own hands. When Nostradamus found her, she was, in her weakened state, busy sewing herself into a death shroud. Her future seemed grim, so she gave up.

We live in a world plagued with lifelessness. People are giving up. They are picking up the needle and thread and are busy sewing a protective covering around their lifeless existence. But then, there are those, who in spite of the smell of death around them, are able to conquer and move on.

A few years back I visited the site of the Oklahoma City bombing. A number of us piled into a car and we made our way to the site of the bombing. After we parked the car and started walking, an anger began to well up in me as I looked at the destruction around me. I thought to myself, "How could he? How could one man dare to do such a thing?" But my anger soon turned to hurt as I approached the actual center of the bomb blast. A large chain-link fence had been temporarily erected to keep people at a distance. And that fence had become a memorial of sorts. Family members, friends, and complete strangers had left flowers and pictures and poems and ribbons. I made my way around the block reading everything. Soaking it all in, I was moved to tears. And then I came across a simple posterboard. A man who had lost a loved one had taken a permanent marker and had drawn a picture of a cross. It was no work of an artistic genius, no masterpiece by anyone's stretch of the imagination, but it didn't need to be. For under that simple rendering of the cross, he had written these powerful words: "Because of the cross I can forgive Timothy McVeigh. Because of heaven I'll make each day." Victorious living is only possible when we live our lives in view of the cross.

Overview of the Text   We've come to a climax in Jesus' ministry. We are well into the third year and for the first time the disciples will clearly confess who Jesus is—the Messiah, the Son of God. This must have been thrilling for the boys. What had only been imagined in whispered tones is now laid out on the table for all to see. He is, in fact, their liberator king. Yet no sooner than Peter gets these words out of his mouth, Jesus raises the stakes. He informs them that their king would be killed in their capital city. It blew their minds. Just when they come to know who he is, they realize they haven't a clue.

The Rock on Which We Stand

 ✳ Make a list of all the confessions of Jesus' identity in the Bible. Place an asterisk (*) by those most meaningful in your life.
 ✳ How did the kingdom Jesus established differ from what the Apostles expected?
 ✳ Recount times when suffering was victorious. These can be either personal or historical accounts.

Meaning of the Text

Some questions are monumental in and of themselves. "Do you take this woman to be your lawfully wedded wife?" "Do you swear to tell the truth . . . ." "Where were you on the night of . . . ." But often the question heightens the dramatic magnitude of the moment. The question Jesus asks his disciples here creates just such a situation.

In our text Jesus is going to ask his disciples a critical question. They have been with him now for more than two years. They really should know the answer. Such a momentous occasion merits a special location, so Jesus has led them north to Caesarea Philippi. This was outside Jewish territory. They knew something was up. Suddenly he turned and asked, "Who do people say that I am?" "Well, opinions vary," they said. "But most land on some kind of prophetic description. You know, a John-the-Baptist type. Or perhaps even an Elijah or Jeremiah." Obviously Jesus knew what the opinion polls showed. This question was merely to get them all on the same page. Here comes the piercing question, "Who do *you* say that I am?"

Peter, characteristically, answers for the whole. "You are the Messiah, the Son of God." The first part of his answer was standard Judaism. That is, Peter believes that Jesus is the coming king—the anointed one—who will lead them to liberty and usher God back into Jerusalem. The second half of his answer is a bit more surprising. To call someone the "Son of

God" was to say he shared God's characteristics and authority. That's a big step for these Jewish boys. They have crossed a serious line here in their awareness of the person of Christ.

Jesus jumps right on it, "You're exactly right." Because Peter recognized Jesus' exalted status, Jesus recognizes his. "Your new name is 'rock' and on you my organization will be founded." Now this is a far cry from calling him the Pope. But let's be honest, Jesus did give him the keys. In fact, he has the power to declare sins forgiven (cf. John 20:23) and beat down the gates of Hades. We see the fulfillment of this in Acts. It was Peter's testimony in Acts 2, 8, and 10 that opened the gospel respectively to the Jews, Samaritans, and Gentiles. He will do there, essentially what he just did here—declare Jesus' identity. Such a revelation is mind-blowing. It demolishes strongholds and establishes a kingdom.

What an exciting moment for Jesus. At last, they understand. The cards are on the table, and they can see the whole deck. Jesus is not merely a clever Rabbi, he is the long-awaited Messiah. Peter too is pretty jazzed. He was the first to articulate this new vision and was duly rewarded. (You can sense his head swelling.) He gets the keys, authority, and even a new nickname, a very manly one at that! The moment is electric.

This next scene (vv. 21-23) reminds me of my Algebra class. Every now and again a new concept would click for the whole class. You could be blinded by all the light bulbs going off at once. The students were delighted, the teacher was proud, and all of life seemed right. Then our teacher, with excitement shooting from his eyes, introduced us to a brand-new concept. The celebration came to an abrupt halt. You could hear the air brakes squealing in our cranial cavities. Ideas collided, confusion ensued. It was mayhem.

So also here. As soon as they grasp the idea that Jesus is the Messiah, he introduces a new concept to them. Namely, that very Messiah would die in Jerusalem. A suffering

The Rock on Which We Stand

Messiah . . . does not compute! How could the one sent to liberate us be conquered by our enemies? They were beside themselves, especially Peter. With his newfound authority he steps way over the line. He takes Jesus aside and begins to rebuke him, "Now you simply must stop talking like this!" It didn't take long for Peter to realize he himself wasn't "all that." Jesus gives him a second nickname: Satan. The pendulum of praise can swing just as far in the other direction.

What they could not see was that the victory of God is carried out at odds to the strategies of men. Jesus did come as a conquering king. His enemy, however, was much larger than the Romans. It was sin itself and all it encompassed: shame, judgment, the devil, addictions, death, and evil. Jesus came to eradicate the consequences of the fall. He came to reestablish communications behind enemy lines. His only weapon was the cross. The very instrument of his demise was the great offensive of God.

There is no way these boys can grasp it. But they need to at least hear it. In fact, they will hear it over and over. Jesus will repeat this prediction some half dozen times. Even then, they will watch with consternation as it is carried out. It won't be until the ascension of Jesus and the descent of the Holy Spirit that they will fully understand how grand is this plan.

It is easy to understand how they missed it. After all, there wasn't a lot of preaching in the synagogue that highlighted a vanquished liberator. Their ignorance is somewhat excusable . . . what about ours? We clearly see that Jesus conquered death through the cross. We fully expect him to come back on a white stallion in battle array. So far so good. But what about the in-between time? Does the concept of conquering through the cross still come as a surprise to us?

Allow me to introduce you to two gargantuan ideas. (1) *Jesus calls Christians to conquer.* We are to conquer sin, principalities, rulers, powers, and ideologies. We are winners!

The Person of Jesus

Yet most of the talk in the church depicts us as beleaguered underdogs. Peter has passed on the keys of his preaching, and we should be on a full-scale assault against the very gates of hell. Nothing will prevail over the church of Jesus. That is his promise. Yet we continue to wallow in our guilt and shame. We continue to submit to worldly addictions. We continue to ask for forgiveness rather than claiming the liberation Jesus promised. We are winners who pretend to be losers.

(2) *We conquer through the cross.* When Jesus died on the cross for us, he was modeling a way of life, not merely enacting a one-for-all sacrifice. Jesus was showing us how to win. Through self-abnegation and sacrifice, we will find resurrection and life. How strange it is that we continue to envy the power, wealth, and ways of the world. No wonder we are still losing; we are using the strategies of the losers. The church lusts for authority of CEOs, the money of investors, the fame of actors, and the power of politicians. When one of these folks is converted, we make a trophy out of them and brag about their contribution. Jesus told such folks they weren't welcome until they resigned all that made them delicious in the eyes of the world. They had to be born again!

This text is not merely a description of Jesus; it is a call to the Christian. Until we die, we will never live. Until we are sacrificed, we won't win. Only through a cross does the Christian conquer. It is our subversive strategy of victory.

Imitating the Person of Jesus

1. As a group, make a list of all of the names given to Jesus in the New Testament. What do the names convey in regard to his identity?
2. Tell the story of the first person you met who was really sold out to Jesus.
3. As an individual, make a list of all the things from which Jesus has freed you. Who is he to you? Reflect on that list, and it will help you explain him to unbelieving friends and family.

The Rock on Which We Stand

About the Authors

Mark Moore is Professor of New Testament at Ozark Christian College, teaching in the areas of Life of Christ, Acts, and Bible Interpretation. Mark did his undergraduate work at Ozark Christian College. He went on to earn a Masters in Education from Incarnate Word College in San Antonio, Texas, while pastoring a bilingual church there. Later he earned a Masters in Religious Studies from Southwest Missouri State University. He returned to Ozark to teach in the fall of 1990.

Mark is the author of a number of books, including other works on the Life of Christ: a two-volume set entitled *The Chronological Life of Christ*, and the more devotional *Encounters with Christ*. He is a popular speaker for both adult and youth conferences.

Mark makes his home in Joplin, Missouri, where his favorite place is with his wife, Barbara, and two teenage children, Josh and Megan, who both know and honor the Lord.

Jon Weece is currently ministering with Southland Christian Church in Lexington, Kentucky. He began in the summer of 2000 on the Teaching Team and as an Adult Discipleship Associate. Jon has served four years as a missionary in Haiti.

He graduated with a Bachelor of Biblical Literature degree from Ozark Christian College in Joplin, Missouri. He and his wife Allison live in Lexington. Jon enjoys a good Sunday afternoon drive, cooking steaks on the grill, reading a good book, and fishing for fish as well as for men.